Ten COMMANDMENTS OF INVESTING

Ten COMMANDMENTS OF INVESTING

Guiding Principles from the Greatest Investment Wizards

SAN ENG | TIM ENG | OIA ENG

MANJUL

Manjul Publishing House

First published in India by

MANJUL

Manjul Publishing House
•C-16, Sector 3, Noida, Uttar Pradesh 201301 – India
Website: www.manjulindia.com

Registered Office:
•2nd Floor, Usha Preet Complex, 42 Malviya Nagar, Bhopal 462 003 – India

Distribution Centres
Ahmedabad, Bengaluru, Chennai, Kochi, Kolkata,
Hyderabad, Mumbai, New Delhi, Pune

Original English language edition published by
Morgan James Publishing.

This edition first published in 2024
Second impression 2025

ISBN 978-93-5543-344-2

Cover design: Christopher Kirk
GFSStudio.com

Printed and bound in India by Repro India Limited.

Disclaimer

Though the authors made every effort possible to give the readers accurate information throughout the writing process, neither Morgan James Publishing nor the authors assume any responsibility for any errors or changes after publication. The contents of the book are the sole expression of the authors and not of the publisher. No person, company, or any entity compensated the authors or the publisher for mention in this book. The authors, to the best of their knowledge and abilities, believe the information and interpretation provided to be correct and reliable, but the accuracy and correctness believed are not guaranteed in any way. Furthermore, the authors assume no obligation to provide updates to the information provided.

The authors are not registered financial advisors. The authors are not, in any capacity, providing professional legal, financial, or investment advice. This book mentioned specific company names, asset classes, and investment strategies for informational purposes only, none of which should be deemed as recommendations to the readers. Reading this book does not in any way establish any fiduciary relationship between the authors and the readers, and the readers should always seek out professional advice from registered financial advisors for all financial and investment decisions. The authors do not assume any liability to any party for any loss, damage, or disruption caused by errors or omissions, whether such error or omissions result from negligence, accident, or any other cause whatsoever. The readers are responsible for their own choices, actions, and consequences in relation to all investment decisions.

This book contains "forward-looking statements" within the meaning of applicable Canadian and U.S. securities legislations. Forward-looking statements and information include, but are not limited to, statements with respect to future asset prices, potential financial crisis, potential economic expansions and contractions, potential for increase or decrease of public debt, the positioning of the authors' portfolios to capitalize on current and future market conditions and outlooks, competitive uncertainties, and various contingencies. Forward-looking statements are subject to various known and unknown risks and uncertainties out of the control of the authors and publisher, all of which may cause results, performance or achievements that may deviate materially from those expressed or implied thereby, and are developed based on assumptions about such risks, uncertainties, and other factors set out herein. No forward-looking statement can be guaranteed, and actual future results may vary materially. Accordingly, readers should not rely on forward-looking statements provided and should do their own due diligence when making all investment decisions.

TABLE OF CONTENTS

ACKNOWLEDGMENTS

We, the authors, are grateful to hundreds of family members, friends, colleagues, and Investment Wizards who contributed their insights and wisdom, and their generous time, support, and patience to help make this book possible. We enjoyed writing this book immensely, having not only learned a lot, but also emerging as wiser investors while making many new friends along the journey.

Firstly, we would like to thank San's parents—Oia, Tim, and Chloe's grandparents—for instilling in all their progeny a respect and love for education and life-long learning. Both grandparents contracted COVID-19 early in 2020 and, sadly, took Grandma from us. Grandpa not only survived but is now in the best shape of his life. We are sad we cannot share this book with the both of them, but we know they are proud of this milestone, particularly Tim and Oia taking co-leads to research and write the book at such young ages. A special thanks also to Oia's 15-year old sister,

Chloe, who created the Wizards logo, the book cover, and all the wonderful portraits of the Wizards and authors in this book. Thank you to Oia's other sister Bella for her work in producing the wonderful book trailer videos.

This book would not be possible without the wisdom from the hundreds of Investment Wizards we researched, worked with, and interviewed. For those Wizards we did not meet or interact with directly, we thank them for the generous sharing of their insights and investment advice through their books and podcasts. For the many Wizards we worked with directly, such as Kathy Xu, William Bao Bean, Joelle Faulkner, John Ruffolo, Eva Lau, Dr. Evan Fraser, Bobby Lee, and so on, we thank them for the privilege of doing so, and for their teachings. Still many other Wizards gave generous time to be interviewed for the Wizards Learning Series—thank you, Alvin Wang, Alex Liu, Paula Madison, Brian Leonard, Willie Smith, Logan Freeman, Victor Li, Dan Ives, Caio de Andrade, Kai Wu, Ken Gee, Paul Moore, James Eng, and many others we cannot list due to the publication timing. We appreciate and have captured their insights on the Wizards podcasts, YouTube channel, and website.

We have a small team of dedicated interns that helped with both the book and the Wizards website. Irene Hung spent countless hours to help create the Wizards site and social media channels from scratch into a thriving, vibrant community of students who are serious about smart investing and financial independence. Colter Shelly helped create and seed much of the quality content for the community.

We would like to thank author Dan Brown, who gave generous advice and encouragement to help with the direction of this book. Thank you also to David Hancock and his team at Morgan James Publishing for their early interest and confidence in our project.

Last but not least, too many friends, alumni, and family friends to name generously offered to read manuscript drafts, providing valuable feedback to shape the book. These include alumni friends from the University of Pennsylvania and Wharton, Columbia University, NYU, Shanghai Jiaotong University, CEIBS, Phillips Exeter Academy, Loomis Chaffee, Taipei American School, and more. We also thank many of San's FF fraternity brothers for their insights and sharing.

INTRODUCTION

The *Ten Commandments of Investing* is the result of a decade-long romance with investing—a labor of love for the authors. We researched the secrets of the world's top investors, the "Investment Wizards," including thousands of books, journals, and research papers. We interviewed hundreds of the brightest macro thinkers and Wizards across the globe. We practiced these investment strategies with our own capital, sustaining many painful losses in our learning journey, but improving our strategies and returns each year.

This book started as research we compiled for self use in an unpublished book called *The Investors Bible*—100+ pages summarizing the wisdom of 55 Investment Wizards. When we shared the *Bible* with friends and family, most found the book to be a useful, concise reference source to learn what goes on in the minds of the best investors. Many early readers were professional investors who gave practical feedback, and they suggested new books to read and more Wizards to research.

Three important discoveries led to the creation of this book, the *Ten Commandments (or "10Cs").* First, we realized that the Wizards share similar investment principles and strategies despite their diverse backgrounds, asset types, and geographies. Second, the initial set of Wizards we studied consisted primarily of older, western white men—not representative of today's diverse global investment talent and markets. Third, the Wizards sometimes gave seemingly incomplete, outdated, or even contradictory advice. We wanted to give our community of serious investors a powerful yet simple and practical guidebook with consistent, actionable principles they could follow, one that could be applied across global markets, asset classes, and strategies.

From this in-depth research, a convincing pattern of guiding principles began to emerge. The more Wizards we studied, the more we found that they share common philosophies and principles that made each of them superstars. To be exact, we discovered the *Ten Commandments of Investing*—a set of 10 guiding principles practiced by the world's greatest Investment Wizards. The 10Cs are applied by the best investors in human history—across many asset classes and investment strategies, in many geographies over many decades. We believe both professional and non-professional investors will find value in the timeless, proven 10Cs.

With COVID-19's lingering impact on the world and our livelihoods, we felt a sense of urgency to improve the book and make it accessible to as many people as possible. Thus, we deepened and accelerated our research to include Wizards from across the globe. We sought to research more female investors, investors of color, and investors focused on alternative asset classes[1] and strategies. Our list of researched Wizards is now nearing 100 and growing. We built a web platform (https://wizards.institute) to publish our learnings, share our interviews with Wizards, and network and learn from other people across the globe. Our goal is to make Wizards Institute the #1 community for learning the principles of smart investing, and an ongoing resource for readers of this book and serious students of investing.

We are honored to work with the respected publishing house of Morgan James Publishing. A cross-generational effort by San (a retiree), Tim (a young professional), and Oia (a student), we believe the 10Cs captures the wisdom of the greatest Wizards while being accessible and practical. At the end of the book, the authors each share how they develop their own investment strategies and portfolios utilizing the 10Cs, with more cases and live support provided in the Wizards Institute online community.

The Chinese phrase for *crisis* 危机 consists of two words: *danger* 危 and *opportunity* 机. We live in unprecedented times, with the trifecta of geopolitical, economic, and health crises—three massive and disruptive forces that are changing forever how we live, learn, love, travel, play, and work. These are indeed dangerous times; but, for the prepared, the turmoil brings greater opportunities. Armed with the *Ten Commandments*—the collective guiding principles from the world's best investors—Wizard students will be well-poised to invest wisely and profit.

Welcome, and thank you for joining us on this fantastic journey to become Investment Wizards!

The Ten Commandments of the Bible

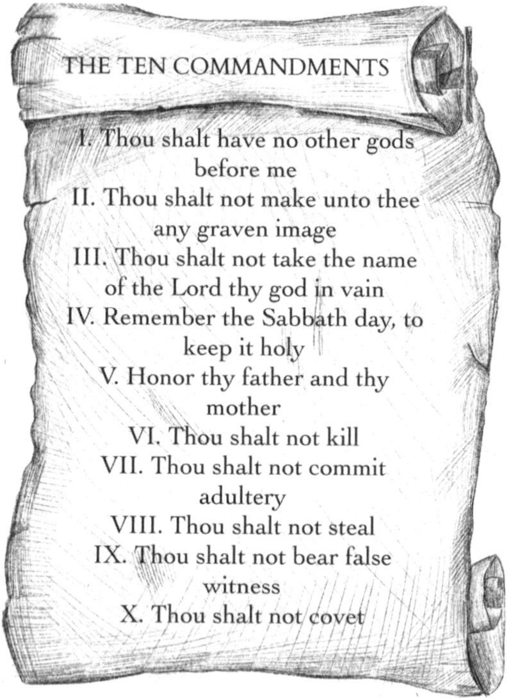

The original Ten Commandments are a set of biblical principles related to ethics, morals, and worship. They are cornerstones in Judaism and Christianity concerning fundamental matters such as God, family, property, law, citizens, and community, and they have guided the conduct of billions of people.

The biblical Ten Commandments are not fixed rules or laws—rather, they are written as general principles with room for interpretation. Thus, they are meant to be applied universally, across changing circumstances, with details to be worked out according to the situation. Furthermore, the Ten Commandments were said to be "written with the finger of God," with its uniquely terse style, so they can be displayed on a single page or stone tablet, shared easily with followers. Inspired by the biblical Ten Commandments, we developed the *Ten Commandments of Investing* from the collective wisdom of the world's greatest Investment Wizards.

The Ten Commandments of Investing

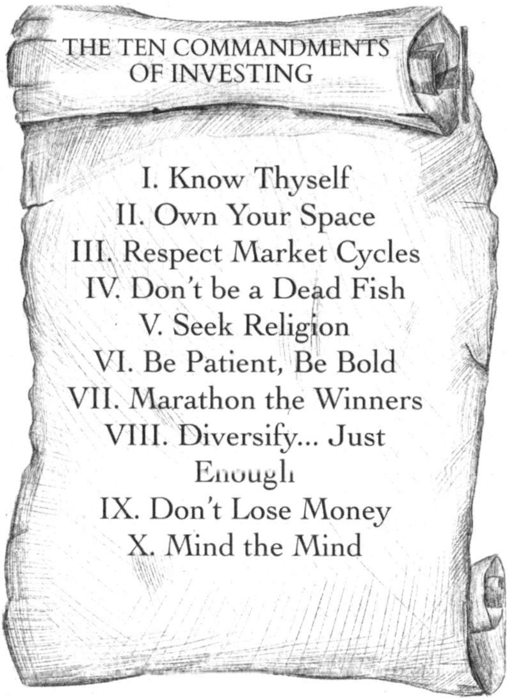

There is no one investment "god"—in fact, there are many Investment Wizards of all ages and genders, investing successfully with diverse strategies across multiple assets classes around the globe. Regardless of which Wizard and strategy, we have discovered that they all share the 10Cs as guiding principles to their tremendous success.

Who are these Wizards? They are legendary names like Warren Buffet and Charlie Munger of Berkshire Hathaway. They are the founders of some of the most popular investment strategies today, such as John Bogle who pioneered the passive index fund. They include the top hedge fund[2] investors like George Soros and Paul Tudor Jones. They are the worlds' top real estate investors such as Sam Zell.

We also learned from the world's most successful venture capitalists, such as Kathy Xu and Zhang Lei. Beyond professional investors, we also studied several genius entrepreneurs, such as Jeff Bezos and Elon Musk to see how they invest in themselves and their companies to achieve their bold missions. We studied emerging markets pioneers, such as India's Ambani of Reliance/JIO, and Hong Kong's "Superman" Li Ka Shing. Collectively, the 100+ Wizards we studied manage tens of trillions of assets, and each are at the top of their game, not just for a year or two, but consistently over decades. For example, Berkshire Hathaway has earned an annual return of 20.5% since Buffett's takeover in 1956; Paul Tudor Jones has returned 26% over two decades. For the full and growing list of Wizards we continue to study, please join https://wizards.institute and subscribe to our newsletter.

Like the Bible, we hope our *Ten Commandments,* written with the help of the minds of many Wizards, can be applied universally by investment students of all ages and skills to great investment success. The Ten Commandments of Investing are intentionally written to be terse, easily understood, and practical for novices, yet packed with wisdom for experts. The authors—San, Tim and Oia—also follow the *Ten Commandments* to develop their own investment strategies and portfolios, with many real cases accessible by practitioners on the Wizards community website. It is our hope that our readers and Wizards students across the globe can find value in the 10Cs to help them become smarter investors, achieve financial independence, and perhaps join the ranks of the Investment Wizards.

According to the World Bank, almost half the world lives in poverty, and the majority are financially challenged, lacking basic financial knowledge and investing skills. In a survey by the Federal Reserve (the Fed) in 2013, 47% of adults have trouble coming up with $400 in emergency funds based only on their savings.[3] We see this in headlines daily as COVID-19 continues to ravage our world: families cannot afford food, medicines, or rent payments without government assistance. Our book and its companion website, https://wizards.institute, develop and share the highest-quality content related to the best practices of smart investing and financial independence for our community of students. We hope to help millions of people live better lives through the practice of the *Ten Commandments of Investing.*

How to Use the 10Cs

For readers with no business or investing backgrounds, the idea of investing, not to mention learning and following the footsteps of the world's greatest Investment Wizards, can be daunting. Do not worry. We have done the heavy lifting to digest hundreds of investment books and thousands of investment papers and articles, and we have interviewed, and even invested with, these

Wizards. Thus, we believe the content should be meaningful for novices and experienced investors alike. That said, we have taken pains to explain each Commandment and concept in simple language, with ample stories, anecdotes, and cases so that even a teenager, as long as he or she is a serious student of investing, can readily understand and enjoy the book. Any investor, whether beginner or professional, will be able to follow the 10Cs and benefit from the collective wisdom of the Wizards.

This 10Cs can be broadly organized in three categories:

1. ***Part 1—Seek and Ye Shall Find:*** Commandments 1-2 help readers think through and develop a long-term investment strategy that suits personal goals and expertise, and build basic habits to become great investors;
2. ***Part 2—Finding Religion:*** Commandments 3-6 help readers understand market cycles and emotions, and conduct proper investment research and diligence, in order to find conviction (religion) in their investments;
3. ***Part 3—Being Devout and Disciplined:*** Commandments 7-10 help readers properly manage their portfolio to reduce risks while maximizing returns consistently over many years, like the Investment Wizards.

We propose a three-step approach to use this book and the 10Cs:

1. ***Read the book, learn the 10Cs.*** Like the biblical Ten Commandments, we have written the 10Cs of investing

in a terse, easy-to-understand style. We provide ample stories and visuals to illustrate key points.

2. ***Go deeper; join the Wizards Institute community.*** We have made available online all the Wizards summaries from *The Ten Commandments of Investing*, so if you would like to better understand Ray Dalio or Kathy Xu, you will find summaries, interviews, podcasts, and discussions from each Wizard. You can post questions for other students, the authors, and even Wizards to join the discussions.
3. ***Most of all, carpe diem.*** Take action—follow the 10Cs. Each Commandment is a standalone principle, but, when taken together, they give us the key steps to investment mastery.

Now without further ado, let us start the 10C journey.

Commandment One:

Know Thyself

Everyone Is an Investor

You are an investor, whether you know it or not. No one told you this at school. You might not even have an investment account. But believe us: everyone is an investor, so this book matters to *you*.

A young teenager may not have her own investment capital, but how she invests her time—to learn or to play—and finds a circle of close friends determine the kind of person she will be in the future. No matter how much wealth they have, adults also make investment decisions every day when they choose to invest their hard-earned income—in cash, in entertainment, in a mortgage, in their education, in the stock[4] market, in a business, or in a retirement account.

Two percent (2%) is the target annual inflation rate set by the U.S. Federal Reserve, the central bank controlling economic growth through interest rates and monetary policies.[5] If you earned $100 today and swept it under the rug, the same $100 note will lose two dollars in value one year later. Five years later, it will only be worth approximately $90 in today's value. By holding cash, you have decided that you are okay with an annual return of negative 2%.

The US treasury bond[6]—a "risk-free" investment because the US government very likely will not default on its debt—will return 2% to you annually in normal times. Ideally, the treasury bonds will match the inflation rate, so you have a nominal return[7] of 2% (and a real return[8] of 0%). Riskier investments, like stocks and real estate, may at times under-perform bonds' stability, but can provide more attractive returns in the long run if market growth is healthy and you invest shrewdly.

Money *can* buy you happiness. According to Twenge and Cooper's research, representing 44,198 adults from 1972 to 2016, the correlation between income and happiness has steadily risen among those 30 years or older.[9] The happiness of people without a college degree deteriorated, while those with higher education and income remained steadily happy. Another study by Nobel Economist Kahneman indicates that the emotional well-being of a person increases until his or her income hits a certain magic number—$75,000 in 2010 (more today, accounting for inflation).[10] Considering that, in 2017, less than 10 countries had a per capita GDP above that threshold, most people in this world would stand to benefit from better financial literacy.[11] We hope this book will further that goal by teaching smart investment principles, improving standards of living and happiness.

So, since we are always investing, why not be great at it? Between the choice of -2% return on cash and at least a 2% long-term return by investing in assets, who would decide not to invest?

Tap Dance, Don't Work

Investing can be daunting at first. The financial jargon, the uncertainty, and the volatility can make it seem like a casino that's impossible to beat. However, there are Wizards everywhere who learned the ropes of investing and developed effective systems to consistently do well in the markets. Much like how pro athletes love their sports and die-hard musicians can't live without their instruments, great investors all share common *passion* and *enthusiasm* for what they do. In most cases, their passion is so great that they even share their philosophies with the world.

Warren Buffett

You cannot talk about investing without mentioning Warren Buffett. With a net worth of $77 billion, Buffett is perhaps also the world's most well-known billionaire miser—he orders the same three breakfast items from McDonalds (never spending more than $3.17), drives a 2014 Cadillac XTS, and lives in the same house he bought in 1958.[12] He also signed the Giving Pledge to dedicate 99% of his wealth to charitable causes. So, you know that at age 90, his 56th year running Berkshire Hathaway, Buffett is not doing it just to make more money.

Buffett loves his job and has been encouraging other people to "tap dance to work." In fact, he started investing at the age 11 and still does it today! Omaha, Nebraska is normally a very small town, but every year 40,000 people fly in to listen to him and his partner Charlie Munger happily share their timeless wisdom. When work is your passion, you love it. It is no longer work—it is fun.

Buffett is not alone. Michael Steinhardt, who achieved an annual return of 24.5% between 1967 and 1978, advises to "always make your living doing something you enjoy: devote your full intensity for success over the long-term."[13] Kathy Xu, the "Queen of Venture Capital in China" and the number two woman on the global 2020 Forbes Midas List of investors creating the fastest growing companies, told us that she cannot imagine doing anything other than what she is doing now. As an investor, Xu loves to grow businesses with visionary company founders; why would she quit doing something she loves?

Celebrities Nicolas Cage and Mike Tyson—and Michael Jackson, when he was alive—"tap dance" to do what they are famous for. They share many things in common, but one may surprise you out of all—they all filed for bankruptcy after they became famous and wealthy. In fact, 60% of NBA players go bankrupt within five years of retirement, and about 78% of NFL players either go bankrupt or experience financial stress after two years of retirement.[14] These people are world class at what they do for work, dedicating much of their time to perfect their craft. Yet, they fail to bring the same dedication when it comes to managing their finances.

The wealthiest of us can still go broke. By 65, you want to have enough in your retirement account to support yourself without burdening others. Tap dance to work; your future self will be immensely grateful if you bring this attitude when you plan for your financial future. For a goal as important as this, everyone should at least spend some time defining how they want to get there.

Six of Our Favorite Warren Buffett Quotes

---

1. ***On Earnings:*** "Never depend on single income. Make investment to create a source."
2. ***On Spending:*** "If you buy things you do not need, soon you will have to sell things you need."
3. ***On Savings:*** "Do not save what is left after spending, spend what is left after saving."
4. ***On Taking Risk:*** "Never test the depth of the river with both feet."
5. ***On Investment:*** "Do not put all your eggs in one basket."
6. ***On Expectations:*** "Honesty is a very expensive gift. Do not expect it from cheap people."

The World Is Cruel

Jeremy Grantham, the British investor with over $100 billion AUM[15], claims that individual investors have two chief advantages over the professionals: "The biggest problem for professionals is dealing with career and business risks: protecting their own job as an agent. The second curse of professionals is over-management caused by the need to be seen to be busy."

Unlike professionals, individuals are not under threat that a quarter of under-performance will lead to investors withdrawing their money (and possibly the loss of their job). No one will criticize you for doing nothing because you cannot find any good opportunities in the market. Individuals will fare much better waiting patiently for the right opportunities and not paying attention to what others are doing.

Jeremy Grantham

A helpful illustration of the competition that exists in the world can be found in the story of "The Good Pig":

> "So I went to Ireland, and my car broke down. Luckily, a farmer was nearby who invited me in for dinner while I waited for a mechanic. Walking around the premises, I saw a pig with only three legs. Surprised, I asked him, 'Excuse me, why does your pig only have three legs?"
>
> And the farmer said, 'Oh, well, see, this pig here's name is Paddy, and let me tell you a story about him. One day, I was out on my tractor when something went wrong and the tractor accidentally got turned over. I was going to be crushed and would have died, 'cept Paddy here ran over and dragged me out. He saved my life that day, he did.'
>
> And I said, 'WOW! That's amazing! So he lost a leg while rescuing you?'
>
> And the farmer said, 'No, but let me tell you a story. My son was fishing in the pond when, all of a sudden, he fell right in. And somehow, his foot got trapped in a reed in the pond. He would've drowned to death if Paddy hadn't run outside, untangled him, dragged him out from the pond, and applied snout-to-mouth resuscitation. He saved his life that day, he did!'
>
> And I said, 'Incredible! So that's why he has only three legs?'

> And the farmer said, 'No. But let me tell you a story. My daughter was getting water from the well. All of a sudden, she fell right in! And she screamed and screamed, but no one could hear her. She would've died, 'cept Paddy here ran outside and rescued her. He saved her life that day, he did.'
>
> 'Unbelievable! But why does he have only three legs?'
>
> And the farmer said, 'Well, you wouldn't eat a pig that special in one go, now would you?'"

What does this story mean? The investment world can be cruel and ruthless: it is "eat what you kill," and most people will act in their own interest. This applies to "professional" advisors with Ivy-league degrees and fancy titles in spacious offices, or the talk show hosts you see on CNBC and Bloomberg.

Only you know and have your best interest at heart. Let's say you entrust your money to a professional hedge fund manager. Before they make you any money, they'll take a 2% cut of your investment as a management fee—plus a whopping 20% performance fee, or profits. To justify that kind of fees requires good returns! Though a manager's interest may seem to align with yours, the performance fee can also encourage the professionals to take outsized risks to enlarge their share of the profits.

Likewise, the brokerage house[16] that gives you the "latest and sexiest" investment tips does not help you make the best investment decisions. They sell you hot tips because they earn money on commission; every time you trade, they get to skim a little off the top. The more you trade, the more they make. As well-intentioned as they can be, you can bet financial advisors will have their own interest before yours.

It can only help to take a more cynical view of the world. Protect yourself by knowing how you are invested (what assets, geography, or strategy), even if you have a professional advising you. In the next subchapter, we will introduce a way for you to find the investment strategy that has your own interest at heart.

Investing Is Personal

Every investor has unique objectives, passions, talents, resources, and risk tolerances—so there is no "one-size-fits-all" strategy. Benjamin Graham, the father of value investing and mentor to Warren Buffett, taught that one of the most important principles in investing is to know what kind of investor you are.

Benjamin Graham

Graham would first ask whether you are "passive or active." Active investors devote time and energy to becoming better investors by doing quality, comprehensive, hands-on research, and hoping their good, hard work will translate to good returns. If this is not your cup of tea, then you can save yourself some work and time by taking the passive approach.

Passive investing involves buying index funds, which track a basket of companies to mimic the performance of the entire market. You will not be beating the market with passive investing, but you will not be under-performing either. Your returns will simply match that of the market, which will grow over time with the real economy. This book talks about both, with more focus on active investing.

Next, Graham would ask whether you are an "investor" or a "speculator." An investor looks at an asset as *part* of a business and himself as the *owner* of the business, while the speculator sees himself playing with expensive pieces of paper that have no intrinsic value. For the speculator, value is determined only by what someone will pay for the asset. It is key that you know what you are investing in; otherwise you are no different from a gambler, leaving your bets entirely to chance.

In this book, "investments" refer to longer-term positions that are decided and managed through fundamental analysis, the careful examination of the asset's financial statements, and growth prospects. Within this realm of fundamental investing, however, there exists as many investment strategies as there are unique fingerprints. Investing is highly personal, and every investor should address these eight questions to develop his or her own strategy:

1. ***Objectives:*** What are your goals? Are you young and can take more risks to grow capital, or are you hoping for more stable income from interest and dividends?
2. ***Interests:*** What are you interested in learning? Investors typically make the most money by focusing on areas they understand and are ideally experts in.
3. ***Style:*** How active do you want to be? Being active requires more time and work. If you are passive, you still need to devote research to ensure the quality of the manager or fund in which to invest.
4. ***Skills:*** What skills do you have? Do you have a background in accounting, medicine, technology, or real estate? Anything to help you evaluate deals in a space?
5. ***Timing:*** Are you a short or long-term investor? Do you need the money soon to pay for your children's education, your retirement, or your home?
6. ***Risk:*** How much risk can you take? REITs[17] (Real Estate Investment Trusts), multi-family apartments, bonds[18], or dividend stocks can be safer than growth stocks like Tesla.
7. ***Asset:*** What asset class do you understand or enjoy learning about? Evaluating different assets can require you to learn new ways of thinking about their profit models
8. ***Place:*** Which geographies are you comfortable learning and investing in?

Regardless of the answers to the questions above, one of the many magics of investing is you can invest in anything and everything. Investors have made millions, even billions, investing in many types of assets, no matter how popular (e.g., Apple or Tesla) or esoteric (e.g., bitcoin or insect farms) across industries, markets, and geographies. There is an infinite possibility of investment strategies. No matter your style, it should be reflected in the eight factors above. It is only through time, focus, research, and learning that one becomes more knowledgeable, and gains an edge in investing.

In the penultimate section of this book, "Ten Commandments in Practice," San, Tim, and Oia have answered these eight questions to help the readers develop their personal investment strategies. There is also a Do-It-Yourself (DIY) sheet that will help you sit down, answer the eight questions, and determine a personal investment strategy.

Given that it is possible to profitably invest in anything, an investor should do some deep soul searching to figure out his or her interests and investment strategy. The next commandment—**C2: Own Your Space**—will build upon these ideas, and highlight that expertise only comes with the time and dedication to any Wizard's areas of passion.

Commandment Two:

OWN YOUR SPACE

You Can Be a Wizard

No one is born an Investment Wizard. Nature does play its part (i.e., Wizards all likely have at least average intelligence), but it is nurture that makes them exceptional investors. You do not need to be a genius to be good at something; you just need to focus and put in the work.

Charlie Munger

Buffett's business partner, Charlie Munger, puts it this way: "The only way to win is to work, work, work, work and hope to have a few insights." Everyone can get lucky and strike a gold mine, but Wizards put in hard work so they can find gold mines over and over again. For you to "own your space," Munger advises:

1. ***Constant learning:*** Be a voracious reader—become wiser every day.
2. ***Ask:*** If you want to get smart, the question you have to keep asking is, "Why, why, why?"
3. ***Be fluent:*** Develop fluency in mental models from the major academic disciplines.
4. ***Be prepared:*** You cannot take advantage of opportunities without preparation.

Malcolm Gladwell introduced the concept of the "10,000 hours rule" in his book *Outliers*, pointing out that The Beatles put in an estimated 10,000 hours of practice playing in Hamburg in the early 1960s, Bill Gates put in 10,000 hours of programming work before founding Microsoft, and the most talented violinists put in 10,000 hours of practice by age 20. By dedicating significant time to their practices, they became experts in a given field.

While the 10,000 hours rule is more art than science, it should be generally expected that the more work you put in, the better you become. Can you become an Investment Wizard in your niche? Absolutely. Start early and stay focused. Let's break down the "10,000 Hours to Wizardry":

The Road to 10,000 Hours

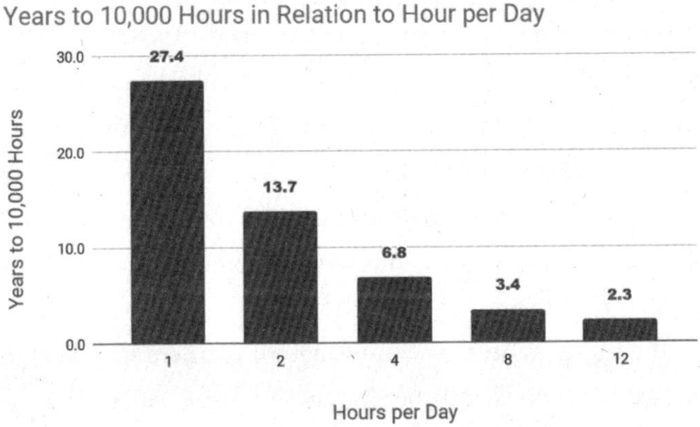

If you take your time, doing only an hour a day, you will master a trade in just over 27 years. While 27 years sounds like a very long time, it is actually plenty of time for serious investors to learn and grow their wealth. For example, 99.7% of Buffett's wealth was generated *after* he was 50 years old. Oia is 17, and she has been spending at least an hour a day to researching, interviewing, and writing for this book. If she loves it and continues for two to three hours a day, perhaps taking some business classes in college, she can become a Wizard in her chosen niche before she turns 30! If, by chance, your full-time job is related to finance and investing, where some positions entail 12 to 16-hour work days or longer, you may well become a Wizard in two years.

You do not even need the full 10,000 hours to start talking intelligently about a topic. Business coach Josh Kaufman explains that people learn new things most quickly in the first 20 hours.[19] In beginner's math, you learn counting, operations, and perhaps some algebra—some of the most crucial foundational tools you need when you move on to geometry or calculus. You also see this when you learn a new language. The first 20 hours you may spend learning some basic vocabulary, grammar, and syntax. You may not understand anything, but within the first hours, you will acquire the tools and fluency you need to deepen your learning, whether by learning more vocabulary or practicing in conversations. You can become fluent quickly and become an expert over time.

The same process applies to investing. There may be some terms or concepts in this book that you don't understand right now. That is completely normal. You may be asking yourself, *What is a bond? What is an option? Who is Warren Buffett?* That too is normal. The hardest part is getting started. Within the first 20, 100, or 1000 hours, you will develop fluency in investing; you will understand the basic terminologies, asset classes, and strategies. Then, all you will need to do is perfect your craft and walk forward on the path to wizardry.

A mathematician does not need someone to explain to him why some infinities are bigger than others. A Spanish native does not need a translator when touring Barcelona. When you become knowledgeable in a field, you no longer need "experts" to guide you through the process. You feel at home and own your space. You have developed *Independence of Thought*.

10,000 Hours Applied

We have ample examples from the real estate space. San's friend, Mike, worked as an engineer for 20+ years. He enjoyed his job but wanted to reduce his salary (W2) income taxes, so he started investing in real estate. Putting in only one to two hours a day over two decades, Mike bought, rehabilitated, and rented out multi-family houses. He learned the ins and outs of investing in real estate while maintaining a full-time job, accumulating 100+ houses in his spare time. He never needed outside capital, using his tax savings from the house investments to refinance and buy more properties. Now a real estate Wizard, Mike has retired from his job, lives off his passive income, and dances to "work" only a few hours a week.

Many high-income earners, who want passive income, actively invest in multi-family housing. To learn why three retired NFL players (Brian Logan, Logan Freeman, and Willie Smith) chose this path and became real estate Wizards after their athletic careers, visit the Wizards website to hear their podcasts and interviews. Our site has ample quality content from experts in this area including Ken Gee—a top property manager/investor, Victor Li—a former pension fund manager on real estate, Joelle Faulkner—CEO of AreaOne, one of the largest farmland funds in world, Paul Moore—who invests in multi-family and other workforce housing, such as mobile home parks, and James Eng, whose firm has financed billions of these great investment assets. They all focused on real estate, taking only a couple of years (or longer, if part-time) and are at their top of their trade after 10,000 hours applied.

The "10,000 hours rule" applies to all industries. John, one of San's classmates, joined a global investment bank as a telecoms research analyst post-graduation. He toiled 10 to 12-hour days, including weekends, as young analysts often do. In just three years, he became the number one ranked telecom analyst covering that country.

Over the next five years, John continued to focus on this trade and expanded his geography to be a regional analyst; he also added the Internet sector to his scope. He proceeded to become the number regional telecom and technology analyst, often interviewed by investors and financial TV channels. With his Wizard status and media stardom, John was able to start his own ten-figure fund, becoming very wealthy while investing in the sectors and regions he loves.

Another friend, Alvin Wang, became a global expert on "XR" (Augmented Reality/Virtual Reality) and artificial intelligence working as President of HTC China, a top VR/AR firm. Dr. Evan Fraser has focused on agrifoods as a professor at a famous agriculture school, the University of Guelph, as well as running the Arrell Food Institute. He is a sought-after speaker and advisor on all things climate change and foods.

Caio de Andrade, one of Brazil's most successful serial entrepreneurs, is now leading that country's digital transformation as President of SERPRO, a US$3 billion organization with a staff of over 10,000. Growing up in Harlem to Jamaican parents, Paula Madison climbed the corporate ranks in Hollywood to be one of the most senior minority executives in Hollywood. After retiring from NBC, she is now a partner of a family investment group focused on real estate, and CEO of Madison Media, a media consultancy with global reach. Paula owns or has owned The Africa Channel and the WNBA team LA Sparks, amongst other notable investments. (To learn more about these individuals' 10,000-hour journeys and how they achieve Wizardry in their trades and investment philosophies, please find their podcasts and YouTube at https://wizards.institute/)

Even passive investors should put in some work. If you wish to buy and hold a stock market index[20] for ten years, for example, you should still research which markets, indices, and managers can generate good returns. For example, San invests passively in multi-family apartment buildings in the US—these are wonderful investments that pay high (8%-12%) dividends, along with the upside of appreciation that can typically earn 1.5 to 2.0 times the capital within five years. Not bad returns for safe, passive investing when you pick the right managers and the right assets in good markets.

However, assets and managers (and their integrity) can vary. So, while these are passive investments, one must still do the homework to evaluate the people and ask the right questions. Lunch becomes tastier and cheaper if you put in the time to find and screen both managers and assets, and this applies to all investments.

Whether it is one or ten hours a day, it is a matter of staying focused and putting in the time to achieve Wizard status. If, like Mike, you have a job unrelated to your investment space, you can become a Wizard part time over more years; if, like John, your job is your passion, you can do so in many fewer years. The sooner you start, as in Oia's case, the sooner you get there!

Independence of Thought ("IOT")

Objectivity and rationality require independence of thought. Remember: just because other people agree or disagree with you does not make you right or wrong—the only thing that matters is the correctness of your analysis and judgment. As you spend more time developing knowledge in your area of expertise, you will begin to have an area of competency, enough knowledge to start thinking critically about investments, and the ability to tell what is right from wrong. If you do not think for yourself, and blindly follow the hottest trends in the market, you will likely get average or worse performances (more on this in **C4: "Don't Be a Dead Fish"**).

In today's frenzied social media world, there is information overload with many news sources to choose from. Most major news outlets are not objective, their views colored by the editors' political and business interests. Even *The Economist*, one of the most respected English-language magazines in the world, is prone to delivering news from a Western-centric perspective.

This applies to highly-compensated advisors as well. When San was 28, as CEO of a fast-growing Internet startup planning an Initial Public Offering,[21] he consulted a number of stock exchange executives and investment bankers from New York, Hong Kong, and London to assess the best place to list the firm. All three places had their merits and disadvantages, and advisors each provided compelling reasons to list in *their* city. Only by doing the homework was San able to compare and develop an IOT on what was best for the company's unique situation, independent of the motivations of advisors and brokers. As in the story of "The Good Pig," we cannot blindly trust third parties.

Take one of San's favorite investments, Tesla. On any given day, you can find fiery Bulls vs Bears[22] that love or hate the stock. Billionaires and famous investors can make convincing cases either to invest in or short[23] the stock. News headlines spit out sensational titles to click-bait the audience. Spend an hour searching Tesla news to read both sides and you will end up more confused than before.

The only way to be comfortable in your position is to develop IOT, and you can only achieve this by doing the work. San has driven a Tesla for three plus years and he understands their products intimately. He reviews all new Tesla technology and products (e.g., their Autopilot software). He reads all the arguments, pro or against, including occasional click-bait articles, to see how they impact the minds of retail investors or "fly-by-night" Tesla traders (the "herd"). He loves long-form podcasts, having himself interviewed top Tesla bull (e.g., Dan Ives[24]) and bear analysts to keep himself up to date (you can find these interviews on the Wizards site). He reads up on competitors and overseas markets, including developments in China, the biggest electric vehicle (EV) market.

By doing all this, he is able to gain conviction on Tesla as a long-term buy and hold and ignore the daily high volatile nature of the stock. Being right 100% of the time is not the point, as no investment is 100% without risks. Tesla is a young, risky firm, and San may still lose money investing in it. However, the key is that his investment thesis is firm, and this conviction should give him a good chance of profiting as long as the thesis remains valid.

It need not be a complex story like Tesla. Remember that Wizard Peter Lynch once said, "Never invest in any idea you cannot illustrate with a crayon. Only invest in what you understand." Whatever asset you choose to study, whatever investment strategy you follow, whatever niche it is—whether it is

Asian telecom and internet like John's interests, or investing in multi-family houses like Mike or Tesla like San—stay focused, do the work, and develop IOT. Chances are, like the Wizards, you will win more times than you lose.

With IOT, you now own your space. No matter which space you pick, or what investments you choose, you will still need to know that macro factors can impact your investment performance. We will dive into these factors in the next commandment—**C3: "Respect Market Cycles."**

A Perfect Husband

Several men are in the locker room of a golf club. A cell phone on the bench rings and a man engages the hands-free speaker function and begins to talk. Everyone in the room stops to listen.

Man: "Hello?"

Woman: "Hi, Honey; it's me. Are you at the club?"

Man: "Yes, I am."

Woman: "I'm at the shops now and I've found this beautiful leather coat. It's only $2000. Is it okay if I buy it?"

Man: "Sure, go ahead if you like it that much!"

Woman: "I also stopped by the Lexus dealership and saw the new models. I saw one I really liked."

Man: "How much?"

Woman: "$90,000."

> Man: "Okay, but for that price, I want it with all the options."
>
> Woman: "Great! Oh, and one more thing. I was just talking to Jamie and found that the house I wanted last year is back on the market. They are asking $900,000 for it. They'll probably take it. If not, we can go an extra eighty thousand, if it's what you really want."
>
> Man: "Well, then go ahead and make the offer."
>
> Woman: "Okay. I'll see you later! I love you so much!"
>
> The man hangs up. The other men in the locker room are staring at him in astonishment, mouths wide open. He turns and asks, "Anyone knows whose phone this is?"

The moral of this story, as it applies to investing, is to beware of Wall Street and any other experts that have your trust. This is not to discourage you from seeking advice from the "experts." Rather, we want to caution that investors should never take other people's advice on face value. As stated above, each investor has different goals and circumstances, and often the advisors' interests are not aligned with yours—the professionals, for example, are playing with OPM (Other People's Money).

One example is the 2008 subprime[25] mortgage crisis: banks repackaged bad mortgage loans (rated B or below) with clever financial engineering, and then resold the loans to investors with triple-A (AAA) rating, the highest grade you can get. The banks themselves were not investing in subprime mortgages.

They make money when they are able to sell these products and earn a commission. They were playing with OPM. At times, the repackaged loans were incredibly complex. Many investors underestimated the risk that came with these triple-A-rated loans and suffered huge losses when the recession[26] arrived. Not only were some of these bankers peddling products with grossly misaligned interests, they themselves did not understand how to properly analyze these toxic "investment" vehicles.

Be careful when entrusting your money to the experts' advice and their sophisticated products!

Commandment Three:

RESPECT MARKET CYCLES

Markets Always Cycle

Uncertainty itself is a rare certainty in investing. New investors unaccustomed to capital markets may be intimidated by the uncertainty and day-to-day volatility. It is common to see some stock rise or drop 5% or 10% in one day, and some may deem it too risky. However, volatility is an inherent part of investing and, over a longer period, will form market cycles. Regardless of your investment acumen, you will most certainly fail if you do not understand cycles and manage your risk properly. The Wizards know to use cycles to their advantage.

Howard Marks

Tim's corporate finance professor at Columbia once invited legendary investor Howard Marks, founder of Oaktree Capital, as a guest lecturer. Marks shared that "dealing with risk and understanding where we are in the cycle are really the two keys to success." Market cycles, the booms and busts, present an ever-present risk to your portfolio. Each cycle may be different in detail, but an investor who has studied past market performances will know that certain patterns can reveal themselves cycle after cycle. How do you learn about cycles? Charlie Munger said, "There's no better teacher than history in determining the future." Knowing the cycles does not give you complete certainty, but an investor who knows the history behind cycles can tip the odds in her favor.

A good investor should also understand psychology. Because human nature hardly changes, emotions will more often than not be a big component of trends. An investor cannot know the future, but she must have a rough idea of where the market is in the cycle to position herself accordingly and reduce the potential downsides. In his book *Mastering the Market Cycles,* Marks introduces the three stages of the bull market:[27]

Market Cycles and Uncertainty

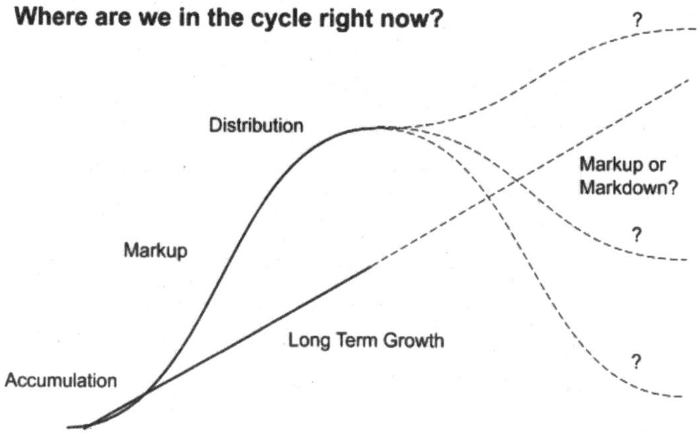

In Stage One: Accumulation, "only a few unusually perceptive people believe things will get better." So, almost no one is investing, out of fear or indifference (e.g., post-Depression between 1930 and 1940, 2001, or 2009). In Stage Two: Markup, "most investors realize that improvement is actually taking place." The market ticks upwards as more people turn bullish. In Stage Three: Distribution, "everyone concludes things will get better forever." FOMO (Fear of Missing Out) sets in, greed takes over, and the market rises until the bubble pops.

Every bull market inevitably must end and go into a bear market; in hindsight, it is relatively easy to see cycles at work.

The problem is that, in the heat of the moment, investors do not know which way the market will go—this is represented by the dotted lines in the graph. You know the economy will grow along the long-term growth line, but the market can go in any direction: up, flat or down in the short term. You can only say in probabilistic terms, never definitely, whether the market will grow or collapse in the near future. "Investing is not black or white, in or out, risky or safe. The key word is to calibrate,"[28] Marks concludes. "Assessing our cycle position doesn't tell us what will happen next, just what's more or less likely. But that's a lot." A Wizard will use what he knows about cycles and the market to allocate his portfolio wisely.

The system of recognizing macro-economic cycles worked well for Marks in 2008. Oaktree Capital lowered its exposure to the market as its analysts believed the economy was on dangerous ground. They used their knowledge of cycles to take precautions. When the market declined, Marks bought. Oaktree raised a $11 billion distressed fund[29] and, in one deal alone, purchased distressed debt that recovered in value a few years later, generating $6 billion in profits for Oaktree investors.[30] Oaktree today manages $120 billion, a testament to Marks' proven strategy.

We will discuss the psychology driving market cycles in the next commandment, and how we may profit from them.

Gauging Market Cycles through Historical PE

A bull and bear market can often be categorized in two different cycles: cyclical or secular.

Cyclical Market Cycles are short term, driven by investor sentiment (not fundamentals), and can last days, weeks, or months. The secular market cycles can span over many years, even decades, and are driven by fundamentals—long-term factors, such as interest rates or earnings.

Secular Market Cycles are characterized by prices rising and falling over the long term. The secular bull market ends when the market is way overvalued, a bubble forms, and a big market correction comes. The Great Depression, the 2000 Tech Bubble, and the 2008 Financial Crisis, mark the end of long-term secular cycles. These massive corrections have made fortunes for astute investors, while destroying wealth of many others.

The most basic and popular way to gauge valuation levels is through the price-to-earnings ratio (PE). The PE is a simple but useful tool to understand how much investors are paying relative to the expected return from the asset. It is calculated by the following formula:

PE Ratio = Price Per Share / Earnings Per Share

As earnings per share go down, or price goes up, the PE ratio goes up. The higher the PE ratio, the higher the implied valuations. If a company has 6xPE, it means that you are paying six times the company's current annual earnings, and it will take the company approximately six years (assuming earnings don't change) to earn back its current valuation.

For high-growth startups that are bleeding money with negative earnings, this valuation method does not work, because you will have a negative PE ratio. However, this measurement can be helpful if you look at the broader markets where many established companies already have solid pathways to profit:

S&P 500 PE Ratios Pre-Crisis vs. Post-Crisis

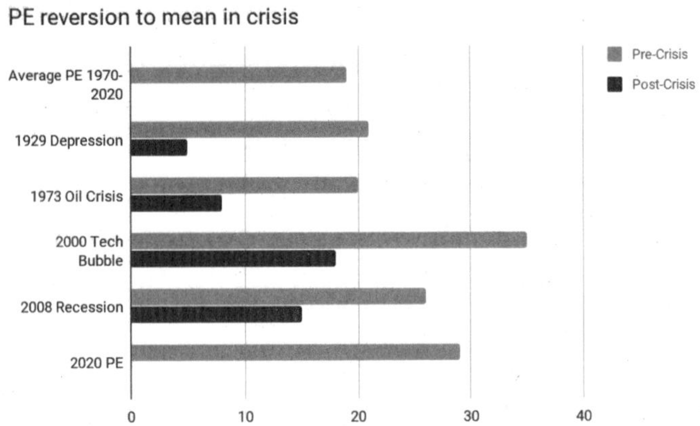

Ed Easterling, founder of research firm Crestmont Research, observes that "a secular bull market starts with a low PE and ends higher over an extended period of time, doubling or tripling the original PE; a secular bear market does the opposite, where the PE stalls and falls by one-third to two-third or more." His observations can be readily seen in the graph above. While high PE ratios can be maintained for a while, an over-stretched valuation cannot grow forever.

The average PE of the S&P 500 has been around 19.4x from 1971 to 2017 (with a median of 17x).[31] Currently, in 2020, the PE sits at around 29x. In each secular bull market, the growth of stock prices outpaces the growth of corporate earnings, leading to a higher PE ratio. This is generally called *Multiples Expansion,* and a smart investor knows that broad market valuations cannot escape the laws of Newtonian Physics of "what goes up must come down."

If the market PE has surged from 15x to 30x to 45x, implying it now takes 45 years of earnings to recoup capital, a Wizard will always keep in mind that the long-term PE average is 19x, and not get carried away by the market's inflated valuation.

Throw out Your Timer

"The problem with market timing is getting the timing right."
Peter Lynch

Every investor should have heard of the axiom "buy low, sell high." If you can buy at the lowest point and sell at the high points of each day, this strategy will indeed make you very rich. Easy, right? Not really. Wizards all agree that timing the market, for the short term at least, is incredibly hard, if not impossible to do so consistently over the long term. Lynch said, "If timing the market is such a great strategy, why haven't we seen the names of any market timers at the top of the *Forbes* list of richest Americans?" That's a great question.

Wait a minute, did we not just praise Howard Marks for timing the market in 2008? Yes, however, Marks was timing the market according to the long-term *secular* cycles, not the short term. Over the six years (2002-2008) for Mark's investment, the market reached a PE ratio[32] of 35x. Thus, the market was clearly overvalued. Marks' $11 billion fund had a long-term investment horizon, allowing him sufficient time to play out the secular market cycle. This insight, investment, and conviction made his fund billions of dollars in just one "bet."

To repeat, we are cautioning against short-term market timing, which is very difficult as this is driven by human emotions, which investors cannot quantify or predict. A longer-time horizon frees good investors from these distractions. Fantastic companies like Walmart, Apple, or Amazon have the potential to become behemoths, even though it was not reflected in the post-crisis market in 2010. We will elaborate more on the benefits of long-term thinking in **C4: "Don't Be a Dead Fish"** and **C7: "Marathon the Winners."**

William Sharpe, the Nobel Laureate of Economics in 1990, argued that market timers are unlikely to produce more than "four per cent per year over the long run." This is because most people are very bad at guessing where the markets will go next and, more often than not, will get the price movement wrong. Unless an investor gets seven out of ten decisions right, Sharpe recommends avoiding market timing all together.[33]

Those are terrible odds. If you see market timing as a coin flip, where the market has a 50/50 chance of going up or down, getting seven out of ten right sounds impossible. Without a "magic" glass ball called "insider trading,[34]" how can you be sure you can consistently get the timing right? How do you know where the markets will go a day, a week, or a year from now?

If you still think you can consistently time the market to profit, heed these words: "There is the Wall Street fool, who thinks he must trade all the time. Not many can always have adequate reasons for buying and selling stocks daily. It was never my thinking that made the big money for me; it was always sitting." Jesse Livermore—widely considered the pioneer of day trading, who took massive short positions during the 1906 San Francisco Earthquake and 1929 Great Depression—said this. So, even a famous data trader is against day trading and market timing. Can *you* realistically do better?

Jesse Livermore

Livermore recognized that trading day to day movements is much harder than investing in longer-term movements. Speculative trading may provide casino-like thrills, but the investor often goes in blind in the next bet. It is great if you love action and do not mind bad odds—but why not just go to a casino? In investing, patience and inaction allow you to think objectively, find the bargains, and invest when the opportunity is right. Invest, do not gamble.

Burton Malkiel, who wrote the influential investment book *A Random Walk Down Wall Street*, asserts that there are no predictable short-term patterns based on charts and past data. Technology made the market "too efficient" for short-term technical signals[35]. You may think you found a unique signal that allows you to profit with market timing when, in fact, it was sheer luck (it is 50/50 for up or down in short trades after all). When too many people follow signals, the signals themselves become irrelevant and self-defeating. As such, market timers will have to keep on developing new strategies to stay ahead in the game. Do not confuse skill with luck!

Thus, use time to your advantage, recognize market cycles, and do not try to time the cycles for quick profits (especially the short-term emotional cycles that are hard to read). That said, as with many things in life, there is a caveat. Market timing is possible, under rare conditions (see the sidebar on Blair Hull.

C4: "Don't Be a Dead Fish" will explore the herd mentality and irrationality that are a big part of cycles; it will show how you are better off being an independent contrarian than a follower of trends.

Market Timing Is Possible (with a Caveat)[36]

Blair Hull

Blair Hull is the founder of Hull Trading Company who served as Chairman and CEO of the firm before selling it to Goldman Sachs for $531 million.[37] He is recognized by *Forbes* as one of "the 40 Greatest Traders of All Time." In the 1980s, he developed his own Black-Scholes-like formula, applying it to find probability in the future and options market. His paper, *"Practitioner's Defense of Return and Predictability,"* laid out the possibilities of timing the markets, and he employs the strategy at his own trading firm. This is what he says about market timing:

1. ***Defining market timing.*** "There is some optimal position of equities and cash that you should have every single day, and that comes out from a variety of information." Simply put, you hope to dodge the bad days and be in the market in the good days.
2. ***Stigma against market timing.*** "Everybody says that... timing the market is dangerous. Well, that may have been true till the year 2000, but with this explosion of data we have had, with new government data, the internet, and even Twitter and social media, we now have a situation where, with new predictive analytics, it is possible to time the market."
3. ***You need an edge.*** "If you were to go to a casino and you didn't count the cards...you are going to lose and that is your disadvantage. If you have disadvantage in all the games you are going to play, my recommendation is that if you are an investor...there's no reason to play... People enjoy the fluctuation. It's a fun game to do. But

not if you're doing it for financial reasons: it's going to hurt you if you don't have an advantage."

4. ***It takes lots of resources.*** "We have a proprietary ETF[38] which we hold as an advantage. We have a proprietary trading system that has servers...we have computers that trade; we don't have people that trade. And we have 25 different servers at the Chicago Exchange, and we're constantly trying to figure out if this server and strategy lost its edge...we're always worried that our strategies are losing their advantage."

So, market timing is *possible*, but only if you have an army of PhDs in math, statistics, and computer science to work on algorithms day and night. You will also need lots of data, computer systems, proximity to exchanges (for faster trade execution), and advanced theories to do market timing effectively. In other words, you need an edge. Without that, stick with fundamentals.

Commandment Four:

DON'T BE A DEAD FISH

Don't Be a Dead Fish

A dead fish will only go where the river flows.

Similarly, a novice investor who relies on others to make investment decisions, whether that be their family or even a Wizard. To consistently do well in the market, you must avoid falling into the herd mentality trap. Just as short-term market cycles are hard to call, market emotions and herd mentality are impossible to predict consistently. Wizards who are aware of market sentiments and opinions often have a big advantage of making profitable contrarian calls, or, at the very least, can protect themselves from losses.

Talk show hosts like Jim Cramer, celebrity host of *Mad Money* on CNBC, and commentators on Bloomberg must sound confident on TV—it is what they are paid to do. It is easier for investors to listen to talking heads than to make their own choices.

But famous people are not immune to being wrong. Cramer, for example, mocked people who were not buying technology stocks right before the 2000 tech bubble crash—those who did not listen saved themselves from catastrophe. On the other hand, in a crisis like COVID-19, some advocated selling out of precaution; others bought during the dip. This time, the "opportunist" profited when the Fed promptly intervened, but it does not necessarily mean the cautious investors were foolish in their actions. Whom can you really listen to? No one, except yourself.

In an experiment published in the *Journal of Behavioral Finance,* a group of students and professionals picked a stock from two stocks that would likely outperform each week for a year.[39] All the stocks offered to the participants were stocks of blue-chip companies[40]. When asked, the students were 59% confident with their skills, while professionals were 65% confident.[41] The students were right 49% of the time, while professionals were right 40% of the time.[42] Amazingly, when professionals were 100% confident in their decision, they were only right 12% of the time![43] Professionals (with their inflated confidence) do not have better odds than you at making the right choices. As the American businessman Norman Ralph Augustine says, "If stock market experts were so expert, they would be buying stock, not selling advice."

Doing what everyone else is doing is easy, comfortable, lazy, and wrong. When the investment goes sour, at least you know everyone else is also suffering. But a herd mentality cannot consistently be profitable long term. If you listened to other people's advice when you bought an investment, how will you know when will be the right time to sell, or what needs to change for your thesis to fail and for you to get out? By not making your own choices, you can never learn from your mistakes and become a Wizard at investing.

Hugh Hendry on Being Contrarian

Hugh Hendry

Scottish investor Hugh Hendry was the founding partner and CIO[44] of Eclectica Asset Management, famed for his 31.2% return in the depth of the 2008 financial crisis.[45] When most were suffering losses, he has gone against market consensus and earned himself the reputation as a prominent contrarian. How did he do it?

Hendry said: "I suspect I am one of the few CIOs who does not maintain daily correspondences with investment bankers and their specialist hedge fund sales team. I am not seeking that kind of 'edge.' Eclectica [his fund] occupies an area outside of the accepted belief systems." He further added, "I attempt to cultivate my own insights and to recognize the precarious uncertainty of global macro trends. First and foremost, I am always preoccupied with the notion that I just do not have the answer."

Hendry defined the three ingredients that make him an outstanding macro hedge fund manager:

1. ***Boldly contrarian:*** Successful but contentious macro risk posturing—this is the real key. It is the ability to establish a contentious belief outside the existing belief system of the broader financial community.
2. ***Favorable risk/reward balance:*** Choose the asset class offering the highest probability of return should the conviction hold true, while offering an asymmetric loss profile[46] should the original premise prove unfounded.
3. ***Strong risk management:*** A best-in-class risk technique that stops losses is the narrative and responds early with loss mitigation procedure—more on this in **C9: Don't Lose Money.**

Meet Mr. Market

Benjamin Graham, the father of value investing, introduced the famous allegory of Mr. Market in *The Intelligent Investor* to demonstrate why the unreliability of market emotions can help contrarians:

Imagine you are a business partner with an unstable guy called Mr. Market. You know your business is worth around $1000 per share. Every day, Mr. Market offers a price to buy your shares or sell his shares of the business. Sometimes, Mr. Market is in a great mood and offers to buy your shares at a price way higher than what the business is worth ($2000). Other times, Mr. Market feels depressed and offers to sell his shares at a super low price ($500). You get to decide whether you want to buy, sell, or do nothing.[47]

How would you want to trade with Mr. Market? It is obvious that you would buy the business when Mr. Market offers $500 and sell your shares when Mr. Market offers $2000. Well, the stock market is Mr. Market (or any other market, such as real estate, commodities, etc.)!

Optimism and pessimism can drive the market valuations too high or too low, depending on investors' outlook. If you look back at the PE chart in **C3: Respect Market Cycles**, the broader market's valuation can often drop more than 50% before starting a new secular bull market. But market mispricing does not only happen during financial crises; individual investments can often be mispriced in normal times too. Graham used the price changes of General Electric (GE) to illustrate this point. We will use Apple, a popular stock today, to explain the price fluctuations in the market.

As of September 1st, 2020, Apple had a $2 trillion market capitalization—the most valuable company in the world. Apple stock in the first eight months of 2020 went from $300 to $220 to $460. How did the value of Apple increase by over one trillion dollars when its business operations did not go through significant changes? Did Apple's business shrink, then double, in reality? While Apple still sells a lot of iPhones, there is nothing truly ground-breaking in the business that shocked investors (though Tim Cook has continued to manage superbly). The answer:

Price (Perceived Value) ≠ Value.

While business operations do not change from day to day, the market perception of the business' prospects can be hijacked by market emotions and irrationality, giving the Wizards opportunities. At the peak and trough of cycles, Mr. Market feels extreme emotions of greed and fear. If you know the market will be irrational at times, you can trade as you would with Mr. Market—buy low and sell high! As Warren Buffett says: "Be fearful when others are greedy, and greedy when others are fearful." The emotional greed and fear often drive the price above and below the fair price. By staying calm and objective, you can take advantage of fear and greed (long-term) cycles.

Jack Bogle, Godfather of Index Investing

Jack Bogle

Investment Wizard Jack C. Bogle was the founder and CEO of the Vanguard Group and credited with creating the first index fund. Bogle preached investment over speculation, long-term patience over short-term action, and reducing broker fees as much as possible. He practiced much of the 10Cs. Here are three of his most important principles in investing:

1. ***Cost Matters Everywhere:*** His formula is simple: "gross market return minus the cost of financial intermediation is the net return." In the long run, the average stock mutual fund returns 7%. When all the fees are subtracted, the net return drops to 4.5%. "If beating the market is a zero-sum game before costs, it's a loser's game after costs are deducted."
2. ***Speculation Costs Everyone:*** By Bogle's calculation, some 99.2% of the market is speculation-oriented trading, as opposed to investment, where firms and individuals hold positions for years instead of nanoseconds. Do not try to beat the speculators. Invest in the intrinsic "enterprise" value of companies and reap their dividends. Find low-cost index funds that can represent investment products such as large company, country-specific, industry-focus indexes.

The Basic Rules Don't Change. Fund managers may have lucky years, but their returns eventually revert to market average. Do not invest based on last year's return. There's always risk in the market; don't try to increase it by timing the market. Adjust your stock allocation as you get older—the percentage of bonds you own should roughly match your age, signifying a decreasing risk appetite as people get older.

Find Your Means

Markets revert to the mean[48]—this is an essential assumption and byproduct of the market's emotional cycles. This financial term suggests that prices can at times swing much higher or lower, but will eventually have to return to a fair, mean value. It is a central tenet in value investing, which depends on buying discounted assets and hoping that price will align with value. You can see it in Marks' graph from the last chapter as well, where the cycle goes above and below the long-term growth line.

Bob Farrell

Bob Farrell, legendary economist at Merrill Lynch & Co., recognizes that volatility is a natural part of the market. While starting with fundamental analysis under Graham, Farrell also employed technical analysis to analyze market psychology to aid his investment decisions. He observed that the market is more irrational than rational, and often overshoots from one direction to another—going from overvalued to undervalued, and vice versa. In addition, market excesses caused by emotions cannot be permanent, but a lot of investors make the mistake of buying or selling at the wrong time—like buying in stage three of the bull market because of FOMO ("fear of missing out"). In short, you (your emotional self) are your worst enemy.

Wizards do not get carried away by market emotions. Investors should instead think independently and use the market over-reactions to their advantage. Assets will eventually revert to a more rational, agreeable "fair" value in the long run, but emotional mispricing triumph in the short run. As investors consolidate their views, some smart investors will recognize the price and value of the assets have diverged so much it creates opportunities for them to buy or sell. Eventually, the market will get the price right.

BFF: Emotion and Long-Term Cycles

In 2008, Buffett famously offered a million-dollar bet to any active fund manager who could beat the market index fund over 10 years. Protege Partners, a hedge fund, took the bait. By 2015, their co-founder Ted Seides threw in the towel, as they were underperforming the index. History shows no surprises. Dalbar's 2017 study found that the active investment fund is constantly outperformed by the S&P 500 market index:[49]

Active Investors Lag Behind?

Equity Fund vs S&P 500 Performance ending 12/31/2016

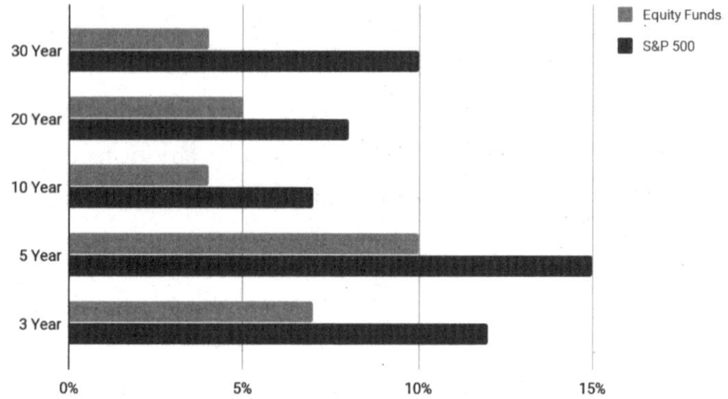

Equity funds returns lag behind the S&P 500 by a sizable margin, regardless of time horizon. This also applies to fixed income funds or even passive index fund investors, and it is also why Jack Bogle founded the Vanguard Group. How can investors be so bad at beating the market?

Dalbar attributed this chronic lag in investor performance to three main factors: psychological factors / market emotions (50%), lack of capital for investing (25%), and capital needed for other purposes (25%).[50] As you can see, the primary issue comes down to emotional mistakes and a lack of capital, allowing emotions to dictate decisions and deploying capital at the wrong time. In other words, people are their own worst enemy. We know from the last chapter that it is a bad idea to time the market, but emotional factors often cause investors to trade at the wrong time, nonetheless. Let's imagine the average investor, Jim, who works a nine-to-five job and has $200,000 saved up in his investment account.

The market is at an all-time high for several reasons (e.g., low interest rates, good economy, no pandemic). Jim buys some more stocks and they go higher. Jim pats himself on the back and congratulates himself for making smart investments. He says to himself, "Great, I just made another 10% in a month. All those people who think this is a bubble got it all wrong. There is no way this market can drop. I love buying and holding!"

When a financial crisis inevitably hits and Jim sees 40% of his lifetime savings wiped out, he tells himself: "Oh, God. I lost 40% because I listened to some bad advice about holding long term. I cannot take this anymore! What if it falls even more? Better pull out while there's 60% left so I can pay for my kids' tuitions and my retirement. I cannot trust the market will rebound as it has done in the past."

Jim, the average investor, shows us how easy it is for emotions to cloud judgement. After all, we are talking about his nest egg. Jim can be right in the bull market and the rally continues; he can also be right to sell his stocks as the market drops further before rebounding. The problem here is that emotions often rationalize positions and dominate investment thinking when they should not. The outcomes do not justify Jim's flip-flop decision making, and he should not let the emotional cycles change the way he approaches his investments.

Wizards understand that the market always reverts to the mean; they also recognize that all investors are prone to emotional faults wired in human psychology (**C10: Mind the Mind**). Do not be fazed when the market overshoots, and you should find opportunities where you can make use of people's emotionality.

Wizards know the importance of staying independent, and they always take other people's advice with a grain of salt, no matter how trustworthy those people might be. Do not make decisions without doing some investigating. If Wizards do run with the herd, they do so consciously—do not be a dead fish! Wizards profit by finding market inefficiencies and making contrarian calls, when others have seriously misjudged the value of an investment.

Next, **C5: Seek Religion** will explore how famous Wizards gain super high conviction for their ideas and why you should too.

Commandment Five:

SEEK RELIGION

Blindly investing in whatever someone else tells you is akin to asking a monkey to hit the bullseye blindfolded. We discussed market cycles and emotions in C3 and C4; they are out of your control, though you can observe and react to them. **C5: Seeking Religion** is about giving yourself control and an edge against the market. It is about seeking strong conviction before you put any of your money at risk. Wizards never make a half-hearted investment; they put full faith in their investment as if they are devout followers of a religion. While there are many paths to financial returns, all Wizards have their own system to help them seek religion, giving them the belief that they are right in judgement. Without "religion," you will only be a speculator, never an investor in the market.

Do Your Homework

It is not a coincidence that the Quantum Fund, co-managed by Jim Rogers and George Soros, generated 4200% between 1970s and 1980s. You get this kind of return by having a systematic framework of analyzing potential investments, not by doing coin flips and hoping the market will do as you hope. Rogers once said, "If you read the annual report, you've done more than 90% of people on Wall Street. If you read the notes to the annual report, you've done more than 95%. If you did a spreadsheet on the annual report, you've done more than 98%."

Soros and Rogers are well-versed in fundamental analysis. They understand market cycles and emotions. They go a step beyond, treating investing like a treasure hunt, looking for signals and opportunities the market has missed. Underlying their performance is a systematic method of analyzing macro-trends, identifying common investor behaviors, and trading against them.

Jim Rogers

Before Japan's economy took off post-1960s, Rogers was one of the first pioneers to see its potential. Japan did become a potential challenger of the US economy until the "Lost Decade" of the 1990s. Rogers' passion for investing in emerging markets extends to the whole of Asia, especially China, and he moved his family from New York to Singapore in 2007. Rogers' faith in the Asian markets was so strong that he was willing to move across the globe to settle in a new city and environment. The move also allowed him to strengthen his faith in whatever investments he would be making in Asia, as he could understand the markets, cultures, and consumer behaviors much better.

Think about the many beginners who trade on Robinhood nowadays. It is very easy to become an "investor" with a few clicks of a button, but how many of them have done careful analysis (on the market, company, product, and earning potential) to tell you with great confidence they made the right call? Or think about the Bitcoin hype in 2017, when some people bought in at the peak of around $19,000 without even knowing how cryptocurrencies work. San, Tim, and Oia have certainly heard many stories from friends who lost money making big bets without knowing what they were investing in.

Do Your Homework—Investor Basics

Without doing the homework, you will always be a speculator. By developing your own method of investment analysis, as well as testing it over time, you will slowly gain religion in your system and find the next potential ten-baggers.

Countless Wizards have authored book after book, teaching other investors how to analyze investments. There is also an endless list of qualities you can look at when analyzing potential investments—so many, in fact, that it would be impossible to cover them all in one book. However, *Seeking Religion*, and the process of doing your homework, really comes down to understanding two things: 1) the qualitative and 2) the quantitative (valuation) of your investment. By analyzing both, you are equipped with the tools you need to find the potential return of an investment and the fair price to invest in it.

Qualitative Analysis

As the name suggests, finding attractive characteristics of businesses is the name of the game in qualitative analysis. As an investor, you will want to find investments with business models that can sustainably grow their top-line revenue and manage their expenses, while maximizing their bottom-line net profits. For each type of investment, you will soon find there are many things you can think about and analyze. However, there are various qualities, like strong brand, healthy distribution channels, and technological advantages, to list a few, that are often loved by investors. These qualities give the investments a known "competitive advantage," making it easier for a company or investment to grow and generate more income and profits.

One much-loved signature quality is known as the moat (a barrier of entry). A moat can come as patent protection, brand name, economies of scale, or network effects, and tends to scare off competition. Think about Amazon's strong delivery capabilities and product offerings, a moat that competitors cannot replicate well. Think about Facebook's 2.7 billion user base; any new social networking site will have a hard time competing against the established Facebook network. Think about Apple and the iOS ecosystem; iCloud/iMessage and all the other functions making it almost impossible for users to switch platforms. A moat makes an investment less risky and creates more potential for revenue and earnings growth.

In summary, you are looking for investments with good qualities (i.e., competitive advantage, brand). There is another sidebar on Anthony Bolton that exemplifies some of the qualities Wizards look for in their investment. An investment with quality will do well in the long term and will not require you to look at its market price every other moment.

Quantitative Analysis

One of the most important tasks quantitative analysis can do for you is Valuation—to determine the range of fair value for which you should acquire an investment. Qualitative analysis starts with the examination of the related numbers—financial statements, revenue growth, number of active customers, units of product sold, etc.—to understand the financial health of an investment and gauge how pricey it is. The following list provides a short introduction for the three financial statements (useful for analyzing any business out there):

1. ***Balance sheets*** give a snapshot of the company's financial conditions. It shows what assets can be quickly converted to cash, how much money the company owes, and its net worth. You'll find the company's liquidity, which provides the flexibility to withstand down cycles

in the economy, pay dividends to shareholders, buy back stock, and take advantage of future opportunities. A good company or investment will have a strong balance sheet to meet its future investment needs and obligations. If the company has way more debt than it can afford, say no.

2. ***Income statements*** tell you how much money the company takes in and spends over a period of time. If a company has a strong balance sheet, you will want to break down the income statement into components and analyze growth trends. It's potentially a good sign when revenue, margins, and earnings steadily grow while costs are carefully controlled.
3. ***Cash flow statements*** show the cash (and cash equivalents) entering or leaving a company. They reflect how much cash the company actually generates—money that is actually *flowing* into and out of the company to meet its debt obligations and other operating expenses.

Quality before Quantity

Watch an episode of *Shark Tank*, and you will know how many different ways an investor can think about a business. A startup may grow quickly but burns a lot of cash unsustainably. The management may manipulate the accounting standards. Wonderful investments are all around you; there are also a lot of bad investments. Great investors think critically about all the "hottest" ideas and allocate their money to grow good businesses.

Kathy Xu

Kathy Xu, the Queen of Venture Capital we introduced in **C1: Know Thyself**, has invested in 80 companies since founding Capital Today in 2005, out of which 17 companies have become the number-one brand in China including, multiple unicorns (private companies with over a billion dollar in valuation). Her continued success cannot be sheer luck.

After talking to JD.com's founder, Liu Qiangdong, for four hours at the first meeting, Xu made an investment that turned her original $18 million stake into $2.6 billion, a 145x return in 10 years. To further grow their expertise in the consumer marketplace, Xu and her team stayed with families in lower-tier cities, which helped them realize that online e-commerce companies were quickly beating offline companies at selling to low-income customers at affordable prices. They concluded that the e-commerce companies like Taobao, JD, and PingDuoDuo would continue to grow, and she now applies her understanding of consumer habits and super platforms to continually look for other companies that can potentially become the number-one brand in their space.

Xu's hands-on research process helps her understand companies above and beyond what normal investors would know. When asked, between a great business idea and a great manager, what is more important, Xu acknowledges that a business idea triumphs even though they are both important. One quality she loves is the Super Platform[51]—an app ecosystem like WeChat or Meituan/Dianpin that provides many services and keeps its users loyal. The Super Platform acts like a moat (see discussion of "barriers of entry" in the last sidebar) that allows the companies to keep growing sustainably.[52]

Most importantly, Xu has a passion for analyzing the qualitative side of a business—especially what it needs to become the number-one brand in their space. With a good qualitative understanding of the business model, company management, competitive landscape, consumer psychology, and many other things, Xu and her team can identify great business opportunities and move on to the next stage—quantitative analysis and valuation to determine an attractive or fair price to pay for the investments.

Like Xu, the top venture capitalists share and practice the 10Cs. John Ruffolo is founder of OMERS Ventures, who led investments of $500 million+ of capital in over 40 disruptive technology companies across North America, including Shopify, Hootsuite, Rover, Desire2Learn, Hopper, DuckDuckGo, Wattpad, TouchBistro, and League. Ruffolo's fellow Canadian investor, Eva Lau, is one of the most well-known entrepreneur-turned-early-stage investors in Canada and North America. She and her husband, Allen Lau, raised $118 million for Wattpad and turned the startup into a global media sensation, with tens of millions of users. Lau currently runs Two Small Fish, a leading early-stage venture fund based in Toronto.

Last not least, William Bao Bean, General Partner of SOSV with $700 million under management, and its affiliates Chinaccelerator and MOX are amongst the most active early-stage venture investors in the world. They all put in more than their 10,000 hours to gain Wizardry in tech investing, including IOT in their niches, and have massive returns to show for their efforts. Their in-depth interviews (podcasts, YouTube) can be found at https://wizards.institute/. We encourage you to listen to how these superstars apply the 10Cs.

Anthony Bolton Quality Checklist

Anthony Bolton

Legendary UK fund manager and investment veteran Anthony Bolton managed the Fidelity Special Situations fund for 28 years. Over this 28-year period, the fund achieved annualized growth of 19.5%, far in excess of the 13.5% growth of the wider stock exchange, turning a £1,000 investment into £147,000 (1979 to 2007).[53] Whenever he meets with the management of different companies, Bolton asks some of these questions to screen potential investments:

1. **General points**
   - What is your business model?
   - Are you vulnerable to changes in legislation?
   - What are the strengths and weaknesses of your distribution channels?
   - How do your products retain their competitive edge?
2. **Strength of a company's franchise**
   - How concentrated is your company's market?
   - How easy is it for a new competitor to break into your market?
   - How big is your company in relation to your competitors/suppliers/customers?
   - Do you have a concentrated or diverse range of suppliers and customers?
   - What is your pricing power?
3. **Sustainability**
   - Where do you foresee the company being in 10 years' time?
   - Will it be more valuable than it is today?

   - What is the sustainability of your trademarks/patents/proprietary technology?
   - What future threats do you predict (not least from your competitors)?
4. **Financial figures**
   - How do you balance cash generation and growth?
   - Can you grow with just the cash your business generates?
   - What are your cash-on-cash returns (cash flow as a percentage of total cash invested)?
   - Do you have enough cash to endure the next crisis?

Beyond the qualities above, it may be helpful to know the ownership structure, the board and key management, and how technology can disrupt the business in the future.

Knowing Your Worth

Christopher Browne's investment company has invested with three of the greatest Wizards: Warren Buffett, Benjamin Graham, and Walter Schloss. How does Browne know when to invest in something? Keep it simple, like shopping in the supermarket aisles! In his *Little Book of Value Investing,* he writes:

"In the meat aisle, you discover that one of your favorites, prime Delmonico steak, is on sale—down to just $2.50 per pound from the usual $8.99 per pound. What do you do? You load up the cart with this delicacy while on deep discount. When you return the next week and see those Delmonico steaks priced at $12.99, you pause. Perhaps this week, chicken or pork might be a smarter buy."[54]

In this story, good investments are found by 1) knowing the intrinsic value (knowing the fair price) and 2) having a margin of safety (buying at a discount). Sounds simple, right? But, as Browne points out, "When the price drops, everyone rushes to buy more of the things they want and need. *Except in investments.*" Everyone loves to look for value in everyday life, but for some reason (e.g., fear), when stocks (or any other forms of financial investments) are cheap, people are more reluctant to look for bargains."

Chris Browne

You cannot know if something is a bargain unless you know its value. You will need to analyze the numbers to find the intrinsic value. When bankers analyze mortgage applications, they first look at the collateral[55] the borrower pledged to secure the loan. Next, they look at whether the borrower has enough income to pay back the loan. The bankers want to make sure they will get their money back, with interest; they judge the riskiness of the loan and approve it for the appropriate return.

You can apply the same principles to analyze other forms of investment: what are a company's assets compared to its debt? How likely is the business going to default? How likely are the earnings to grow? By analyzing the numbers, investors can get a better sense of the right price to pay for an investment.

Please remember that "Price ≠ Value." The best companies cannot be great investments if you buy them at overpriced valuations. Once you find the intrinsic value, you will seek the religion you need to invest with full conviction. (If you want to learn more about valuation, we have included more on valuation basics in the appendix at the end of the book.)

Seek Religion

After doing your homework, you should have found great investments with amazing qualities and have estimated the fair price to buy the investment. But what if you were wrong about the fair price? To overcome this problem, you can follow the paths of many great Wizards (Charlie Munger, Warren Buffett, Walter Schloss, James Montier, Seth Klarman, and Joel Greenblatt) and invest with a "Margin of Safety."

The Margin of Safety is a cushion provided by the difference between the market value and the intrinsic value. In the 1950s, Graham would not buy a company unless it was selling at two-thirds or less of its intrinsic value; so, if the company is worth a dollar per share, he would at most be willing to pay 66 cents. Nowadays, there are probably less of these mispriced companies out there in the public markets (though distortions exist in many other markets, like real estate and other private investments), but Warren Buffett still recommends a margin of safety of at least 25% (which is possible when Mr. Market has terrible days).

There are three reasons why following the Margin of Safety can help you become a better investor: 1) the price can rise 50% and still not be overvalued; 2) you become contrarian and buy when the markets have excess fear; 3) you reduce your downside while maximizing the upside, thereby improving your risk-return ratio.

C5: Seeking Religion is all about developing your investment process to make better analytical decisions. You no longer need to be a dead fish and listen to others' advice. With a system you believe in, you can start to find religion in your investment ideas and deploy your money with full faith. Even if you get some investments wrong, you will learn from your mistakes and continue to refine your system.

Commandment Six:

Be Patient, Be Bold

"It's not what you buy, it's what you pay for it."
Howard Marks

C5: **Seeking Religion** is arguably the meat of this book: you learned the importance of having a system that will help you get "religion" on a potential investment. It is where Wizards spend time doing the heavy lifting and verifying their ideas. Now that you have sought religion in an investment, gained by proper fundamental research to determine intrinsic value, you already know when the right time is to buy. Buy only when the price is lower than your target price. Simply put, the right time is when the price is right.

Right Time = Right Price

We know from **C3: Respect Market Cycles** the importance of respecting and not timing daily fluctuations in the market. We know from **C4: Don't be a Dead Fish** that price is often distorted by many factors, but especially investor emotions, in the short run. Wizards know to wait for the right time to pay the right price.

Always keep Marks' quote in mind when investing, that anyone can make money if the price paid is low enough. If an asset's intrinsic value is $100, pay below with sufficient margins of safety. Even if Mr. Market is super optimistic (valuing it at $200) and the economy looks great, it makes little sense to pay $200. If you had a margin of safety and bought it at $70, or even at $90, you are much more likely to realize investment gains in the long run than if you bought it at over-valued territory. It's simple and logical—but investors often forget this. The key is to resist action bias, the preference of action over inaction.

Let us use soccer penalty kicks to illustrate this point. The penalty taker shoots a ball 10 yards away from the goal; he can fire the ball towards the left, the middle, or the right. Likewise, the goalie has the option of diving left, staying in the middle, or diving left. If the goalie dives in the same direction as the ball, he has a good chance of making a save. Otherwise, the odds are not favorable. In 286 penalty kick footages in elite matches, researchers found that the penalty taker shoots the ball down the middle 30% of the time.[56] It will be beneficial, then, if the goalie also stays in the middle 30% of the time. In reality, however, goalkeepers stay in the middle only 6% of the time.[57]

Why is this the case? If he stays centered (does nothing) and the ball goes in on the sides, the goalie will look foolish. If he dives towards the side and the ball goes in the right, he has, to the observer at least, tried. Paid a high salary, these professionals feel like doing something is better than doing nothing, though doing nothing may help them! Moral of the story: do not do something because you feel like you need to act; it is better to be patient and do the right thing rather than act promptly and do the wrong thing.

A Wizard knows not to buy overvalued assets; he suppresses his itch to do something. He keeps in mind the intrinsic value of the company, following his investment's latest updates and thus its changes in value. He does not let fluctuations, hype, or emotions cloud his judgement. With a long investment horizon, he will only invest if the right price presents itself and if he feels confident about the trade.

Patience pays off. That said, when the right opportunity or right price presents itself, go bold.

Mukesh Ambani and His Reliance Empire

Over the summer of 2020, Mukesh Ambani, Asia's wealthiest man, brought his Indian telecom company, Reliance Jio, on a fundraising spree. Within nine weeks, Jio was able to raise $15.2 billion dollars from 10 prominent investors, including Facebook, Saudi Arabia's Public Investment Fund, and KKR.[58] In what some consider the most epic sibling rivalry in modern corporate history, Mukesh Ambani built a telecom company from scratch that leapfrogged his younger brother Anil Ambani's established telecom business. Today, Ambani's ubiquitous empire spans across different industries—textile, oil and gas, petrochemicals, and telecommunications.

Mukesh Ambani

When their father, Dhirubhai, passed away in 2002, Mukesh and Anil, who were once synergetic business partners, entered a big fight over the control of their father's Reliance Industries empire. Their mother, Kokilaben, stepped in and split the company in two. Mukesh owns Reliance Industries—holding the established, but slower-growing, oil and gas, petrochemical, and refinery business. Anil got Reliance Group—the faster-growing telecom and financial service businesses.

Anil's business was originally fast growing. He rapidly expanded into new industries like the entertainment and film industry, where he soon signed a movie contract with Steven Spielberg's Dreamworks. He also invested heavily in the 2G/3G mobile networks, which in 2008 were the cutting-edge telecommunication technologies (which were quickly replaced by next-generation technology). By 2014, Anil's companies started to get into trouble for the huge amount of debts that they had taken on. With his media ventures falling apart, he was also forced to sell some of his stake in other media entertainment companies to repay debt. (more on debt and leverage in **C9: Don't Lose Money**).

Mukesh, on the other hand, had established businesses that would generate a significant amount of profit and cash flow without requiring a lot more investment in land and equipment. While he always wanted the telecom space and knew that India's future depended on it, Mukesh focused only on what his company was good at and steadily grew his business in those spaces. Plus, there was a 10-year non-compete between the two brothers. So, as much as Mukesh wanted to enter the telecom space, he was forbidden by law to go after his younger brother's business specialties.

Mukesh did not stay idle; nonetheless, over the 10-year period, he learned about the business landscape of the telecom industry, developed a network of lobbyists and informants, and invested in companies that would help him with the eventual launch of his telecom network. He did his homework, seeking religion on his crown jewel. And, in 2016, he rapidly rolled out Reliance Jio's telecom network, engaging in price wars with other mobile operators in India. By 2019, Jio had 30% of the Indian mobile operator market with the goal of capturing 50% by 2025.[59]

Anil's struggling telecom empire became even more at risk under the intense market competition. The sixth-richest person in the world in 2008, Anil lost the business rivalry against his brother and faced bankruptcy in 2020.[60]

Seek religion on your investments. And, when the time and price are right, go bold!

Go Big, Go Bold

If you had invested one dollar with the American hedge fund Wizard Michael Steinhardt in 1967, who was introduced in **C1: Know Thyself**, it would have turned into $481 when he retired in 1995 on the 24.5% compound return.[61] He said, "Don't make small investments—you only have so much time and energy when you put your money in play. So, if you are going to put money at risk, make sure the reward is high enough to justify it." If you have spent the time to do research, determine the asset's intrinsic value, and wait for the right price, go big and go bold on your investments. Make it worth your while.

One of the most famous examples of going big and bold is George Soros' play on the British pound. In the early 1990s, Britain's inflation rate hit an all-time high of 8.1%. The interest rate was 15% and the economy was shaky and bound to crash.[62] By September 1992, Soros saw that the market was completely overheated and a severe down cycle was looming, and he made a substantial bet that the British pound would plummet in value.

George Soros

Soros famously told his head trader, "Go for the jugular," and his fund sold one billion dollars' worth of pound short, flooding the market. The government initially had enough US dollars in reserve to absorb the excess supply of the pound. When this was not enough, Soros called other investors and currency traders and asked them to follow suit. Seeing the weakness in the system, other traders happily complied and continued to sell the British pound. At one point, nearly $10 billion worth of the pound flooded the currency market. Without enough foreign currency reserves, the Bank of England could no longer maintain the currency rate as required by the European Exchange Rate Mechanism—a system to maintain stable value between currencies and encourage trade. As a result, the British had to give up their membership with the Exchange Rate Mechanism and allow the pound to lose its value as people dumped the currency. The value of the pound dropped from US$2 to US$1.5, losing 25% of its value over a few months.

This one conviction investment netted Soros one billion dollars. Soros cited his biggest regret as not being bold enough. He had done his homework, determined the intrinsic value of the pound, and gained religion on the weakness of the British currency system, so he could have bet bigger and made more profits. Of course, this is only true in hindsight. If the trade had gone terribly wrong, Soros could have lost big as well (read about Soros and the Hong Kong currency system in 1998). No Wizard has a 100% success rate in investing. In the case of the pound, Soros' hard work and boldness to challenge the Bank of England allowed him to make a winning trade.

Will our friend Bobby Lee, one of the biggest Bitcoin evangelists, be proven a Wizard like Soros for his early and bold bet on this crypto-asset? Lee has vocally and boldly bet his reputation and career on the future of Bitcoin. We believe it is still too early to tell. (To decide for yourself, listen to his in-depth interview at https://wizards.institute/)

Once you are sure of your investment's intrinsic value and have conviction, you must go big and go bold. A good opportunity does not come often, so act with decisiveness and conviction and seize it when the proper circumstances present themselves.

George Soros: "The World's Greatest Money Manager"

Soros is often mentioned in the same breath as Warren Buffet, though their strategies are different. Buffet is a long-term value investor, whereas Soros is perhaps the best speculative (short-term) investor in history. Soros is a controversial figure, criticized by some for his shorts on currencies and for his open support of progressive, liberal policies. Soros' net worth is estimated at $8 billion, even after having donated more than $32 billion to his philanthropic agency, Open Society Foundations.

Soros' Five Investment Principles

1. ***Take advantage when markets turn chaotic:*** Since markets are emotion driven, investors can profit by seeking and investing when big gaps arise between price and value. "The best opportunities are had by detaching from emotions. Investors should simply focus on market prices and value of underlying assets."

2. ***Preserve capital***: Surviving requires some elements of risk; it is the smart risks that make the difference. Invest only in what you understand and what meets your criteria. Take risks when you feel you have a better and different perspective. Soros is not always active; he knows it is okay to sit on the sidelines, do the homework, and pounce when timing and opportunity are optimal.
3. ***Don't over-diversify, stay focused:*** Focus on a handful of strong assets that have the capacity to produce huge profits, thus offsetting losses from other investments. It's much easier to identify one superstar investment than one hundred. Soros focuses his energy far more intensely on identifying the right investments. When he finds one, he knows the risks of losing money are low.
4. ***Keep quiet about your investments:*** What others think is meaningless to Soros. Do the necessary research and form your own views, particularly in the trading world. There is no need to publicize your trades and trumpet the market's moves.
5. ***Fortune favors the brave:*** When following the above rules, luck is not needed. Markets and values are often disconnected due to human emotions. After doing the homework on an investment thesis, and clearly odds are very much in favor, dive, don't tiptoe in. Finding opportunities missed by the herd—this is how big money is made.

Commandment Seven:

Marathon the Winners

Ride the 10-Baggers

One of the most common and costly mistakes for novice and experienced investors alike is selling the winners too early. Rule #1 for Investment Wizard Peter Lynch's Magellan Fund is not to sell the stock when it has gone up 40%, even 100%. Many investors trim or sell their winners and add to their losers. Lynch advises that if you have done the homework, and if the investment thesis holds true, there is no reason to sell early and miss out on future earning potential.

Peter Lynch

Lynch gave the example of Walmart. Its stock rose 10 times in the first 10 years it went public, yet if you had gotten in at year 11, you would still be sitting on a 10-bagger. As long as the company continues to generate 20% returns on equity year after year, it is not too late. To "rebalance" a portfolio automatically because a stock has risen is a lot like pulling out flowers in the garden to grow the weeds.

Most of the greatest Investment Wizards echo Lynch's views. John Train said, "Don't sell a great stock just because it has doubled. The greatest stocks may go up 20 or even 100 times in a generation or two." Kathy Xu's strategy is to keep all her portfolio companies with 25% or higher growth per annum.[63]

Exceptional companies are rare.

Buffett and Munger know this well: "You should be fully aware of one attitude Charlie and I share that hurts our financial performance," Buffett said. "Regardless of price, we have no interest at all in selling any good businesses that Berkshire owns. We are also very reluctant to sell sub-par businesses as long as we expect them to generate at least some cash, and as long as we feel good about their managers and labor relations."

If you have done your homework, sought religion (**C5: Seek Religion**), waited patiently for the right time and price, and invested boldly (**C6: Be Patient, Be Bold**), why sell it when it has gone up, when it is proving the conviction? Superstar firms are ones that you generally need not worry about. They are long-term industry leaders, often disruptors and innovators with sustainable moats; they do great in good times and bad. Besides Walmart, other examples include Google, Amazon, Apple, Tencent, JD.com, Alibaba and, history will tell, Tesla.

Zhang Lei

Novice investors make the common mistake to "take profit" or "rebalance," while professional investors may be forced to sell for other reasons. For example, for San's $100 million venture capital fund, he invested in 16 portfolio companies. The fund had a "time life—a three-year investment period and a seven-year life to return all capital and profits to investors. This is the structure of most venture capital and private equity funds. Only by showing profits and exits can the fund manager raise a larger next fund. So, there are both structural (time life of the fund) and marketing (to show fast profits for track record) issues pressuring virtually all funds to sell early. For these reasons, San's fund ended up selling a portfolio firm that IPO-ed on NASDAQ early, and selling the private ones on-path to IPO, to show profits, with the "dogs" (worse companies) being left in the portfolio. This is exactly counter to the interests of both the manager and the investors of the fund. This is also why some of the best-performing investors have long-term or "evergreen" funds. Kathy Xu's Capital Today and Zhang Lei's Hillhouse Capital come to mind for great Chinese fund managers with long-term funds, and of course Berkshire Hathaway is famously structured as long-term, even permanent capital.

The Magic of Compounding

"Compound interest is the eighth Wonder of the World."
Albert Einstein

What is compounding and why does Einstein call it the eighth Wonder of the World? Benjamin Franklin explains it beautifully this way: compounding is when "money makes money. And the money that makes money makes more money."

The Magic of Compounding

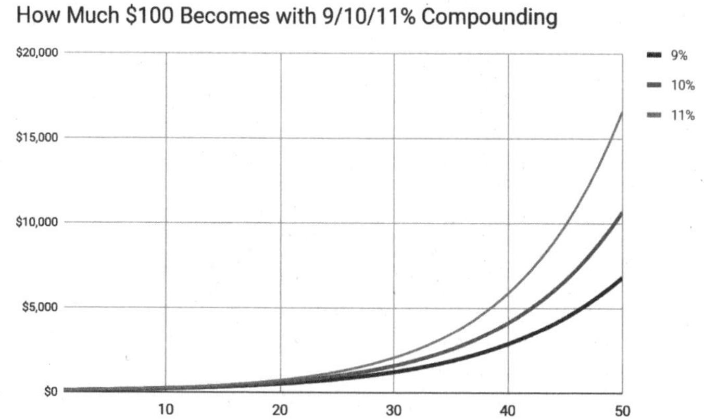

Imagine if you have $100 dollars today. You make 10% each year. After the first year, you will have $110. After the second year, you'll have $121. By the 10th year, you'll have $260. By the 20th year, you will have $672. By the 30th year, you will have $1744. By the 40th year, you will have $4525. And by your 50th year, you will have $11,739. Even though you only make $160 in the first ten years, compounding amplifies the earnings you have by reinvesting the earnings to generate more money over time. Your investments will grow exponentially, because you keep on growing the invested capital.

Each percentage return can make a big difference. Comparing 9% to 11% annualized return, you will find that an extra 2% each year will double the amount in 50 years. So, even though your initial return may seem miniscule, keep growing it over time and the compounding will magically amplify your returns in the future.

Richard Russell

Richard Russell (1924-2015) is considered one of the most influential financial writers of modern times. Why is it important that an investor starts investing early? Russell shares the story of Sally and Jack:

Sally opens an IRA[64] account at age 19, and she invests $2000 annually until she is 26. After seven years, she stops contributing to the account. Jack, who is the same age as Sally, starts contributing $2000 a year at age 26 until he reaches age 65. Assuming the IRA gains an average of 10% (7% interest plus growth), who do you think has more for retirement at age 65? At age 65, Jack has $973,704 in his IRA account, while Sally has $944,641 in her account. At first glance, it seems like Jack won out in the end. But remember Sally put in only $14,000 compared to Jack's $80,000, a full $64,000 less! In addition, Sally grew her original principal by around 67,500%, while Jack's grew by 12,000%. While Sally stopped contributing to her IRA account, she still has income from her job and can potentially continue to save $2000 each year. Although Jack invested a full 33 years more than Sally, Sally clearly beats Jack when you look at the superiority of her investment returns.

So what did we learn?

1. ***Start early.*** Investing early and being patient are very important keys to securing your financial future—you actually don't need a lot of money; you need patience, time, and compounding magic to do its job
2. ***Enjoy the magic.*** Compounding explains why Investment Wizards always marathon the winners, then sit back and enjoy their gains!

Rich Man, Poor Man by Richard Russell

The average investor is not a genius like Bill Gates or Steven Spielberg, with exceptional talents to create tremendous wealth. We instead all need sound financial plans to build our wealth. Russell's four rules of investing can help us towards that goal:

1. ***Rule 1—Compounding:*** To compound successfully, you need the following: perseverance in order to keep you firmly on the saving path; intelligence to under-

stand what you are doing and why; knowledge in order to comprehend the amazing rewards that will come if you faithfully follow the compounding road. And of course, you need time… Remember, compounding only works with time!

2. ***Rule 2—Don't Lose Money:*** Don't lose money, at least not a large amount of money. Most people lose money in disastrous investments like gambling, rotten business deals, greed, and poor timing.
3. ***Rule 3—Rich Man, Poor Man:*** The wealthy investor doesn't need the markets, because he already has all the income he needs. If no outstanding value is available, he waits for the opportunity. He can afford to wait as he has money coming in from different sources. And what about the little guy? This fellow always feels pressure to "make money" and, in return, he's always pressuring the market to "do something" for him. He doesn't understand value so he always overpays. He never heard of the adage, "He who understands interest—earns it. He who doesn't understand interest—pays it."
4. ***Rule 4—Value:*** The only time the average investor should stray outside the basic compounding system is when a given market offers outstanding value. Russell judges an investment to be a great value when it offers: (a) safety; (b) an attractive return; and (c) a good chance of appreciating in price. At all other times, compounding routes are safer and probably a lot more profitable, at least in the long run.

The Rule of 72

American investor, fund manager, and philanthropist Walter Schloss achieved a compound annual growth rate (CAGR) of 15% over 54 years. We can think of few Wizards with such consistent returns over five decades! Schloss is also a big fan of compounding, which he employed to drive his success. He uses the simple Rule of 72, commonly taught in math classes to illustrate the power of compounding.

Walter Schloss

The Rule of 72 says that when you divide 72 by your expected rate of return, you will get the number of years it takes to double your money. So, if you were to invest $100 with compounding interest at a rate of 8% per annum, then 72/8 = 9 years needed for the investment to turn into $200. Incidentally, 8% is the average returns generated by the US stock markets over long periods; so if you were to buy a stock market index, you have a good chance of doubling your money every 9 years—not bad for passive investing as long as you are patient.

Like the Rule of 10,000 in **C2: Own Your Space**, 9 years may be a little too long for some people. But when you think about your investment horizon, had you started investing when you were in your twenties, you can have your money double five times by the time you are 65, which leaves you with 2 x 2 x 2 x 2 x 2 = 32, or 3,200% returns, if you stayed in the market. Furthermore, we have only made the assumption of 8% average stock market return. If you are capable of earning beyond what the market average is, you lower the time it takes to double your money and achieve faster financial growth.

In conclusion, do not sell your winners too early. Marathon them and let the 8th Wonder of World work its magic!

Commandment Eight:

DIVERSIFY... JUST ENOUGH

Stay Diversified

Diversification is the Holy Grail of Investing. That is how Ray Dalio, founder of Bridgewater Associates with $100+ billion AUM, describes the power of diversification, saying that "a lot of people think the most important thing is to find the best investments. That's important, but there's no great one best investment that can compete with something like [diversification]."[65] Yes, diversification will work wonders for you. Diversification spreads your risk by putting investments in different asset types, geographies, and sectors. You should always diversify, but not over-diversify to the extent that you cannot follow your investments anymore. When used properly, diversifying can cut your portfolio risk while maintaining the same level of expected returns, improving your risk-return ratio.

Ray Dalio

Diversification allows you to earn more for the same unit of risk? Sounds like a deal too good to be true. Harry Markowitz, the Nobel Prize laureate, agrees that "diversification is the only free lunch" in investing. Sir John Templeton, pioneer of global diversified mutual funds and one of the greatest investors of the 20th century, adds that "to avoid having all your eggs in the wrong basket at the wrong time, every investor should diversify."

Jack Schwager, the famous author of the acclaimed book *Market Wizards*, has asserted that by simply increasing the number of holdings in your portfolio, you reduce your portfolio's volatility and the magnitude of equity drawdowns (declines). In his book *Market Sense and Nonsense,* Schwager gave the following chart to illustrate the benefits of diversification to minimize risk of portfolio decline:

The Magic of Diversification[66]

Schwager's chart above shows that the probability of a portfolio declining decreases with more assets in the portfolio. If you have

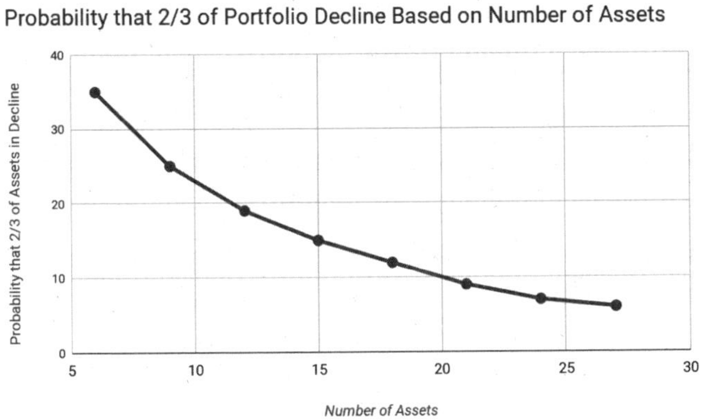

five assets, there is a 35% chance the portfolio will decline by two-thirds in one month. If you add 10 assets, that risk is halved. With 25+ assets, the risk drops to 6%. To make the math work, the investors must hold these three assumptions:

1. The individual holdings are completely uncorrelated.
2. There is an equal chance of each asset winning or losing in a given month.
3. For each asset, the size of wins and losses are equivalent.

Jack Schwager

You can see the risk declines as the number of assets goes up, dropping fastest with the first few diversifications. Most investors assume that diversification benefits beyond 10 are minimal, but Schwager demonstrates that there are still benefits in diversifying after 10 assets, though with declining marginal benefits. According to Schwager, "How many more beyond 10 will be case dependent, but generally speaking, 20 or more will be a better choice than 10 (as long as added investments are of equivalent quality and sufficiently diversified)."

Dalio, after doing similar research, concluded that investors diversify best when they have "15 to 20 'good' and 'uncorrelated' return streams"—with emphasis on good and uncorrelated. Dalio further explains that, when you have fifteen uncorrelated investments, you "can improve your return-to-risk ratio by a factor of five...that's five times the expected return with the same unit of risk!" Simply by picking more (uncorrelated) assets, you potentially earn the same rate of return with reduced risk exposure.

If you take Dalio and Schwager's advice and closely monitor 15 to 20 investments, you can derive great benefits from diversification. However, you can spread yourself too thin when you try to find 15 uncorrelated investments of similar quality. Remember: a significant portion of the Holy Grail's benefits come from the first 15 investments, so you can choose to be less diverse and still enjoy a good amount of the benefits.

Diversification for Idiots?

Consider the following quotes:

1. *Andrew Carnegie:* "The way to become rich is to put all your eggs in one basket and then watch that basket."
2. *Mark Cuban:* "All that asset management, diversification, it's for idiots. Because you can't diversify enough to know what you're doing."
3. *Warren Buffett:* "Diversification is a protection against ignorance...but makes very little sense for those who know what they're doing."

Now, you might ask: whom should we believe? The diversification folks or the contrarians? If you read closely, though, at first brush those three Wizards may sound like they are against diversification—but they are not.

1. Carnegie wants you to look at the basket carefully (**C2: Own Your Space**). You need to know about your basket enough to be sure you never put all your eggs in the wrong basket at the wrong time, ever.
2. Cuban wants you to do your homework (**C5: Seek Religion**). You need to know what you're investing in and have conviction that it can make you lots of money. Keep in mind that Cuban is also a billionaire celebrity, who invests in the NBA teams, movie productions, and *Shark Tank* portfolio companies. He is more diversified than you may think.
3. Buffett wants you to not be ignorant / seek religion (**C5: Seek Religion**). You need to know what you are doing, just as Cuban advocates. Buffett also

owns more than 45 companies under Berkshire, as of August 2020.

Don't Over-Diversify

Both diversification and non-diversification can work in your favor. But as Buffett, Dalio, and Schwager says, diversification is a risk-reduction measure that stops you from putting all your eggs in the wrong baskets at the wrong time. It blocks you from maximizing your returns on your best investment, but also saves you from being a bottom investor, making it safer to grow your portfolio over time. For new investors, diversification makes your rookie mistakes much less costly by spreading the risk across more investments.

However, over-diversifying puts you at risk of spreading yourself too thin. If you do not put in the time to do your homework, you will inadvertently make poor selections for your portfolio. Diversification strategy can vary from person to person, but you should always make sure there is enough diversity in your portfolio to shield you from some of the bad eggs, but not so much that you lose track of your investments.

There are clear risk-reduction benefits to diversifying, and within diversification you can also decide how aggressive you want to be. This chart from Fidelity's *Guide to Diversification* compares the performance of diversified portfolios in relation to their risk:

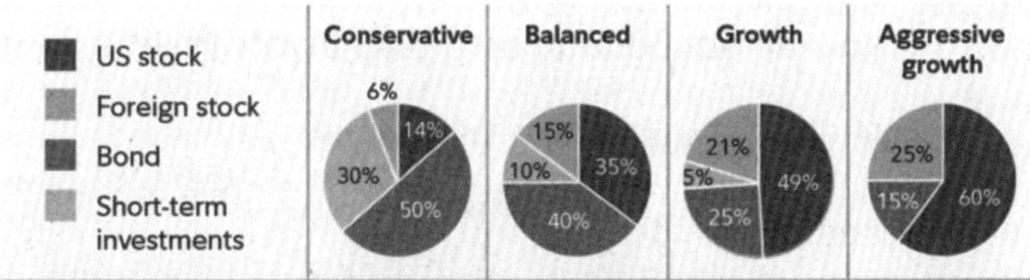

Annual return %	Conservative	Balanced	Growth	Aggressive growth
Average annual return	5.94%	7.93%	8.94%	9.63%
Worst 12-month return	-17.67%	-40.64%	-52.92%	-60.78%
Best 12-month return	31.06%	76.57%	109.55%	136.07%
Worst 20-year return (annualized)	2.92%	3.39%	3.10%	2.66%
Best 20-year return (annualized)	10.98%	13.84%	15.34%	16.49%
Historical volatility	4.47%	9.51%	13.00%	15.68%

If you decide to pursue aggressive growth or high-conviction ideas, your annual return may be greater, but accompanied by high volatility. If you decide to achieve more balanced diversification, you make compromises on maximum return but provide more stability for your portfolio. Only you can decide how much you want to diversify and how much risk you can take.

Sample Portfolio Diversification

You can diversify by picking individual investments or by investing in "total market" index funds. If you do not have enough time, Jack Bogle recommends using passive "total market" index funds to take your share of the market growth in a cost-efficient manner.

Jack Bogle's Three-Fund Portfolio

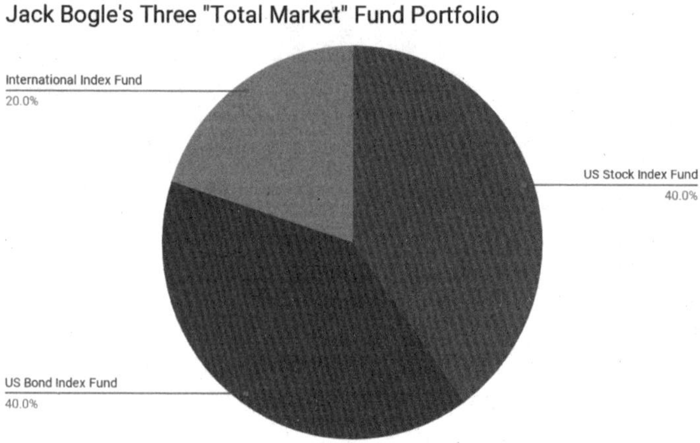

David Swensen, the famous manager of the Yale Endowment fund, likes a wider variety of investments. If you like picking investments, you can consider splitting your investments between active and passive investing.

David Swensen's Model Portfolio

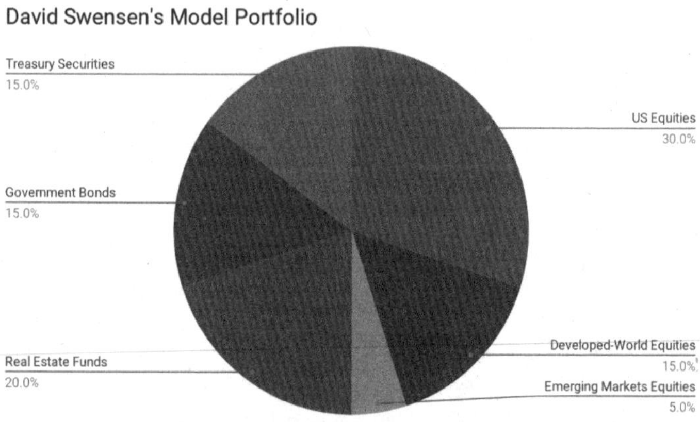

Commandment Nine:

DON'T LOSE MONEY

There is no return without risks and no free lunch (**C8: Diversification** is the one known exception). Remember—the return is only half the equation. More than a few Wizards have advised that the difference between the wise and the foolish investor is that the former focuses on risks, while the latter focuses only on returns. Risks should not be shunned but be fully understood. Take calculated risks and invest aggressively and decisively after achieving conviction (**C5: Seek Religion**). Wizards religiously manage their risks in four ways.

Cut Losses

"It's not the ones that you sell that keep going up that matters. It's the ones you don't sell that keep going down that does."
Warren Buffett

Wizards like everyone else sometimes make bad investments—the key is avoiding big losses that can decimate your portfolio. Wizards are impatient with cutting losses. It is okay to forego opportunities but never okay to suffer permanent capital loss. Cheap markets can get cheaper, and expensive ones can get dearer. While it may seem obvious that you do not want to lose money, why is it critical never to have large losses? The chart below shows how much you need to make, after suffering losses, to return to your original portfolio level:

% Return Needed to Recoup Losses

% Loss	% Gain Needed		% Loss	% Gain Needed
5%	5.3%		50%	100%
10%	11.1%		75%	300%
20%	25%		90%	900%
40%	66.7%		95%	1900%

The higher the percentage loss, the more you will need to generate in gains to return to your original level. At 5% loss, you will only need 5.3% to recoup. At 20%, it takes 25%. To lose 50%, one must regain 100%, and if down 90%, a whopping 900% is needed to recoup. It becomes exponentially harder to get back into the game the more you lose.

Just as **C7: "Marathon the Winners"** advises to keep the winners, the Wizards advise to get out of clear losers before they decimate your returns. Yet many investors, new and old alike, make the costly mistake of holding onto their losers hoping that someday they will break even. Selling losers is psychologically hard as it proves they are wrong, and people dislike being wrong. They think that, as long as they don't sell, the losses are not real losses.

Wizards bear in mind that very rarely do portfolios have 100% winners—even for the best investors. If just one in a portfolio out of 10 gave 5 to 10x return, while the losses of the other nine are cut to a minimum, the overall portfolio would produce handsome returns. Investors just need to control their losses! For example, Buffett cuts losses quickly and decisively. He knows that a loss in the stock market is part of the investment process and the key is not letting it turn into a bigger one to devastate a portfolio. In April 2020, deep in the COVID-19 crisis, Buffett sold all of his $4 billion in airline stocks to cut losses.[67] The reason? He saw that the pandemic—a force majeure event—changed the entire investment thesis around travel and would take years to recover, if ever. So he cut his losses. In May 2020, he began trimming his significant bank portfolio, for similar reasons.

Avoid big losses. Don't let the bad eggs in your basket wipe out all the gains of the good ones.

Margin of Safety

Inherent in **C5: Seek Religion** is the concept of margin of safety. Investors cannot have true conviction unless the entry price is at or below the intrinsic value. Virtually all Wizards we studied champion and practice margin of safety.

Seth Klarman, chief executive of the hedge fund Baupost Group, said this margin protects investors from substantial losses in moribund markets. The investment legend further explained that a "margin of safety is achieved when securities (or any other asset) are purchased at prices sufficiently below underlying value to allow for human error, bad luck, or extreme volatility in a complex, unpredictable, and rapidly changing world."

Warren Buffet is one of the staunchest believers in the margin of safety and declares it one of his "cornerstones of investing." He has been known to apply as much as a 50% discount to the intrinsic value of a stock he invests. For stock investors, we can illustrate with ABC stock. Let's say you have done your homework and determine the intrinsic value of ABC to be $100, which today is trading at $120. The investor may set a limit order[68] for $80—20% below the intrinsic value—and just wait. Since we discussed stock markets cycle up and down, driven by emotions and many factors, ABC may one day trade down to $80, in which case it is bought. On the other hand, ABC may never dip to $80 and the investor may never own the stock. This is acceptable as long as investors have placed similar orders, with margins of safety, with other stocks. Patience eventually will pay off, with investments having sufficient margins of safety.

Your Common Risk-Minimization Tools

Investment Wizards use many tools to prevent big losses. Here are four common ones:

1. ***Stop Loss:*** A stop-loss is designed to limit an investor's loss on a security position that makes an unfavorable move. Once the price falls to a certain point, your investment will automatically be sold to prevent fur-

ther losses if the price drops further. The big advantage is you become very disciplined with cutting losses and minimizing drawdown. However, you usually want to set stop losses at around 15% to 25% of the stock price to avoid accidental stop-losses due to short term market fluctuation.

2. ***Convertible Note:*** In private equity, investors often employ convertible notes to protect themselves from investment risks. The convertible note is a special type of loan that the investor can convert into equity (ownership) of the business. As the loan is safer (more senior to equity), the investor is more protected and may choose not to convert to equity if the investment does not perform well.
3. ***Put Options:*** The put option is like insurance for your investment. The investor and the recipient agree prior to the investment to give investors the options to sell his shares at a predetermined price point (after paying a premium for this option). If the market price drops enough, the investor can purchase shares at a low price in the market and sell his shares at the predetermined price point.
4. ***Collaterals:*** This is especially important in real estate. Lenders usually want to see you have property of value to use as "collateral," so they have assets of value to confiscate if the borrower cannot pay back their loan. Debt lenders—whether a bank lending to borrowers or private individuals or debt funds—often require personal guarantees extending the collateral to the borrower's

other assets for extra security. No matter what asset class or strategy you choose to invest with, always fully understand the downside (how much can you lose) and find ways to mitigate huge losses.

The true story of "Wife-Beater Willie" Billy illustrates points number three and four below. Early in his career, San worked as an investment manager with a multi-billion-dollar private equity firm. One of his first deals was a $16.5 million investment in a Philippines mobile phone operator. San met the founder and CEO Willie, a tall man dressed in blue jeans and a light plaid jacket, who paid a visit to San's Hong Kong office.

While the target investment met all the fund's criteria, San's instincts told him something was "off" about Willie. For one, Willie wore nothing but a white tank-top (what's commonly called a "wife-beater shirt") under his jacket. Willie also contradicted himself several times while presenting his investment case, and, in retrospect, the Fund team should have noticed some of these alarm bells. The Fund's partners decided to move ahead with the investment but only after San's insistence to add a put option to the deal. The put option stipulated that at any time within five years of the investment, the Fund could ask for a refund of the capital plus interest. The put was secured by more than $16.5 million worth of buildings owned by Willie and his family.

Soon after the investment, Willie became uncommunicative and the project experienced many delays. In year four, the Fund decided to exercise its put option, but Willie had disappeared, nowhere to be found in Hong Kong or the Philippines. The money was also gone. When the Fund tried to recover the funds by seizing the properties, they discovered that Willie had already sold these assets. The Fund got both the Hong Kong and Philippines police involved and three years later, Willie was arrested, and the funds were finally recovered from Willie's other assets. Thank goodness for the put option!

The moral of the story? Always structure downside protection. And San would add, trust your instincts and never invest in a founder who pitches in a wife-beater shirt! ;o)

Don't Over-Leverage

The term "leverage" comes from physics, meaning a system or tool that amplifies forces. In investing, leverage[69] usually means investing with borrowed money. Leveraged investing can be a double-edged sword that amplifies both earnings and risks. Much like anything else in investing, you are rewarded greatly when you make the right calls using leverage, but it can also devastate your portfolio due to higher losses.

For example, if you started with $100 and borrowed $100 to buy $200 worth of Tesla stock, a rise in 50% will now give you a return of 100%. Conversely, a 50% drop wipes out the entire portfolio. Beyond a 50% loss, the broker will require you to add more money into the account, or they will sell your equity holdings (they choose what and when to sell) to recoup the loan. One bad call in a leverage investment makes it infinitely more difficult with your losses amplified, as we learned earlier in this chapter.

Li Ka Shing

Li Ka Shing, one of Asia's wealthiest businessmen and investors, dubbed "Superman" in Hong Kong, is a vocal critic of using leverage to invest. During the 2008 financial crisis, Superman warned Hong Kong speculators who had hoped to time the market bottom to not overstretch their finances if they could afford to lose more. *Shark Tank* star Kevin O'Leary also advises most investors to never use leverage to invest in stocks. Buffett, in his 2010 shareholder letter, said that "any series of positive numbers, however impressive the number may be, evaporates when multiplied by a single zero." Too often leverage produces zeroes, and Buffett has repeatedly said that "the only way smart people can get clobbered is with leverage."

Leverage works well to tempt the greedy. If you do use it, please heed the Wizards and do so with extreme caution.

Wrong Even When Right

One year after the 1997 Asian Financial Crisis, the world was on the edge of another global financial crisis. In 1994, John Meriwether, the former vice-chairman and head of bond trading at Salomon Brothers, formed Long-Term Capital Management (LTCM).[70] Meriwether recruited on his Board of Directors Myron S. Scholes, and Robert Merton, who were awarded the 1997 Nobel Prize in Economics for their achievement of pricing derivatives[71].[72] With such big names, investors flocked to invest in LTCM. The fund's core strategy was convergence bond trading. Here is an example (not for the faint of heart but try to follow).

If you had a 29.5-year treasury bond and a 30-year treasury bond, you could basically expect them to be priced the same, unless you thought the US government would default on its debt within the six-month period (very low probability). LTCM found that 30-year bonds were always priced slightly higher because of their higher liquidity in the market (fewer liquid investments are valued less). By shorting the higher-priced 30-year bond, and longing the lower 29.5-year one, LTCM hedges their bet and earns the discrepancies until the prices converge.

In essence, their strategy is a spin-off of arbitrage[73]. LTCM trades a lot of different products using this strategy, including non-US sovereign bonds. The fund was quite successful from 1994 to 1996, earning 20%, 43%, and 41% in their first three years.74 As perfect as the strategy appeared, the spreads (difference) between 29.5 and 30-year bonds were very small, and required leverage to amplify the returns. At the end of 1997, the firm started with $7.3 billion in equity but had held $120 billion worth of assets—a high leverage of 16-to-1.

While normally prices should eventually converge to fair value, we know from **C4: Don't Be A Dead Fish** that market emotions can drive prices in the short run. The following year, LTCM returned some money back to the investors and started the year with $4.7 billion.[75] When Russia defaulted on its national debt in 1998, the fear of another Asian financial crisis spread across the markets, causing a rush from riskier investments to safe havens. Prices immediately rose for the 30-year bond, which LTCM shorted; prices dropped for 29.5-year bonds, which LTCM held long. For both ways of each trade, LTCM was losing money because of short-term volatility. By mid-September, LTCM saw its equity drop down to $600 million.

You would think LTCM would be fine as long as it held these investments for long enough. However, because of the high leverage of LTCM, banks started to worry whether the firm could make the margin call (afford to pay it back). If the banks withdrew their loan, LTCM would be forced to sell its assets and, given its size, would greatly disrupt the financial markets. Even though price would eventually recover, the Fed had to step in because of the size of the debt involved, brokering a deal to get a group of banks to buy out 90% of the firm, and its financial obligations.[76] Even though LTCM had a smart system, its high leverage ultimately caused it to go underwater.

Moral of the story: again, use leverage with extreme caution. If LTCM's superstar elite team got burnt, wouldn't you?

Out Before In

"Every company needs an exit strategy and an exit plan. Ideally, the exit strategy should be agreed upon by the founders before the first dollar of investment goes into the company."
Basil Peters

Peters, the angel investor who was the ex-CEO of a tech company bought out by Cisco, wrote the above quote in his book advising founders of tech companies.[77] The same principle of "Out Before In" applies to investing. Never invest in any asset without a clear exit strategy. In fact, the best investments have multiple exit options. It is critical to formulate and religiously adhere to a clear plan for exit to limit losses while you are still neutral and objective.

For example, in stock investing, savvy investors who have determined the intrinsic value of the stock usually set orders to buy at below that value with a margin of safety, and they may also put in a take-profit order (TPO), which is the opposite of a stop-loss order. The TPO order specifies that a position should be sold if it hits a certain price that is above the investors' view of the intrinsic value, thereby locking in an exit strategy.

We also demonstrated the put option as a stop-loss exit strategy in the previous sidebar. In real estate, smart investors also employ multiple exit strategies. For example, in multiple-family apartment investing, the exit options may include a refinancing (to cash out principle), an outright sale of the entire asset, or a partial sale by converting to condos. The next sidebar illustrates one real case example.

The Out before In principle is logical and is necessary in an overall risk mitigation strategy to cut losses and avoid losing a lot of money.

BRRRR—Multiple Exits (and Infinite Equity Returns)

San and Oia invest in multi-family housing, deploying different strategies. One strategy is called BRRRR—or Buy, Rehab, Rent, Refinance, and Repeat. This is truly an amazing strategy with multiple exit options—and, if done right, infinite equity returns. The crux of their strategy is to focus on undervalued multi-family apartment buildings with value-add potential. We will illustrate this with a recent, real-life example.

Their friend Mike bought a five-unit multi-family building in New Jersey for $290,000, all cash. At the time, the property had only two tenants, and was in need of big repairs. Over the next nine months, Mike spent $100,000 to improve the property, including replacing the leaky roofs and revamping several units.

One year later, all five units of the building have been rented out with over $7,000 per month of rental income. Despite COVID-19 and the poor economy, Mike was able to secure a mortgage from a local bank, who now value the property at $640,000 based on the increased cash flows. The bank will loan 65% of the value or $416,000, while Mike pays 35% but keeps 100% ownership of the building. The existing rents cover the monthly mortgage payments and expenses, with net cash flow of nearly $1,000 per month. Mike pockets $416,000—or $26,000 more than the $390,000 total he invested into the property. As

Mike owns 100% of the property and has recovered all of his principal with a surplus of $26,000, plus net monthly $1,000 income from rental cash flows, his equity return on his investment is truly *infinite.*

The BRRRR strategy offers multiple exit strategies. First, the $416,000 cash-out refinance. Mike could also have chosen to sell the property outright at $640,000. He could also have applied with the city to "condo-mize" the building and sell each of the units individually.

This is why experienced property investors love BRRRR.

Commandment Ten:

MIND THE MIND

Readers of this book and other serious students of investing will likely readily understand the logic and agree with the first nine commandments. After all, the 10Cs are developed from the world's greatest Investment Wizards—they owe their tremendous success by following the same guiding principles across different time frames in history and applying them to diverse geographies, asset classes and strategies. You too, can gain by using the 10Cs.

Like religion, the hardest part is not understanding of the commandments. Devout Christians fully understand the biblical Ten Commandments—it is following through on these guidelines consistently over many years that is very difficult. Consistent execution is key. People encounter rough times at school and at work, with their kids or marriages, driving them to violate the commandments so often taught to them at Bible school or at church. Investing is no different. Most investors—whether beginners or full-time professionals, fail because of this last and perhaps most difficult of the 10Cs, **C10: Mind the Mind**. We describe the three most common and dangerous mental mistakes made by investors and how Wizards overcome them for long-term success.

Control Emotions and Hubris

Most investment mistakes are attributable to ignorance, myopia, and hubris—and principally hubris. Hubris, or excessive pride and self-confidence, means staying within a well-defined circle of competence. It means identifying and reconciling disconfirming evidence and resisting the craving for false precision and certainties. Above all, it means never fooling yourself, for you are the easiest person to fool. Be flexible and humble, learn from your mistakes. Michael Steinhardt said, "Good investing is a peculiar balance between the conviction to follow your ideas and the flexibility to recognize when you have made a mistake."

Wizards advise us to try to contain natural optimism, to stay cool. They also advise us to know our strengths, weaknesses, and limitations. Be aware that human nature will want to win most of the time (leading to, for example, taking lots of small profits), and will dislike losses (leading to, for example, buying more to lower average prices or refusing to sell losing positions). Wizards know that losing is part of the process, so they learn to accept it. In order to have IOT and own a space, investors must do what Wizards do: stay within a well-defined circle of competence. The 10,000-hour rule applies.

Wizards also know that good performances, especially short-term ones, are often due to luck and not scalable or repeatable. Investors must recognize that one of the hardest things to do is to reverse one's thinking, especially if a specific approach or investment has been profitable for a long time. The longer the period of success, the more important the reversal will be.

Last not least, never fool yourself, as you are the easiest person to fool. What feels great is often the wrong thing to do—such as buying on weakness, as it looks to be a better value than last week, averaging down as you overpaid, or taking small profits to feel right, while missing that rare 10-bagger.

Moreover, Wizards who perform consistently over decades distance their emotions from investing. They always keep in mind **C4: Don't Be a Dead Fish** and remember that other people's emotions are their Best Friends Forever. Cheating on them means not following through. Form a sound investment philosophy and strategy. Exercise emotional discipline and adhere to your plan religiously; resist the crowd and do not be part of the herd. If you cannot resist temptation, you absolutely MUST NOT manage your own money.

Despite being hailed as one of the best Wizards of all time, Buffett often says he "exercises humility and restraint" to control emotions and hubris. Similarly, his partner Charlie Munger stresses intellectual humility, "acknowledging what you don't know is the dawning of wisdom."

Once again, *knowing what you do not know is the dawning of wisdom.*

Ray Dalio's Key Advice

Ray Dalio is one of the most vocal, respected, and prolific modern teachers of the markets and investing, as well as life principles. A simple Google search will generate thousands of articles, videos and podcasts with his wisdom. We will not rehash those here. Our biggest takeaway of many from Dalio are as follows:

1. ***Develop IOT:*** Think and work for yourself; come up with independent opinions.
2. ***Stress-test:*** Find the smartest people around you and ask for differing opinions; ask, "Why?" and stress test your conclusions. Don't try to find why you are right (you already know that), and ask enough smart people to find out how you may be wrong (thus avoiding costly mistakes).
3. ***Be humble:*** Do not be over-confident. Hubris can be detrimental.
4. ***Improve:*** Keep learning, especially from mistakes, and keep improving.
5. ***Repeat***

Keep Learning

"An investor who has all the answers
doesn't even understand all the questions."
Sir John Templeton

Every Wizard we studied spent years honing their craft. Still, none of them consider themselves immune to being wrong.

They stay on the learning curve. Everything is constantly changing. The wise investor recognizes that success is a process of continually seeking answers to new questions.

Neil Shen

Neil Shen, who founded and runs Sequoia Capital China, consistently ranks at the global "Midas List" of venture capitalists. In 2020, Shen ranked number one globally, meaning he made more money for investors than any other VC. Shen is known as the "Unicorn Hunter," having invested early in nearly half the most valuable internet companies in China—many of them household names like Alibaba, JD.com, Meituan-Dianping, Didi-Chuxing, Ctrip.com, and even ByteDance, the startup that gave the world the global sensation, TikTok.

Shen attributes his success to constantly learning. He says, "Even a company as successful as Alibaba and Tencent still fears that its existing business model will be disrupted one day...what matters is sticking to core competences and adapting to changes in an ever-changing market." The only way to do that is to start every day with fresh eyes and brain cells willing to learn.

The advancement of technology is making progress come faster and faster. Today, it is not surprising that small companies have the potential to disrupt incumbent leaders, as businesses have to move faster to adapt to consumer preferences. Keep yourself informed of new market trends, and you will be able to find good businesses and opportunities. Being uninformed is like investing blind.

Mind the Mind

The Wizards recognize that the psychology of staying calm and disciplined is a critical success factors for the long haul. Here is collective advice from the Wizards on how to *mind the mind*:

1. ***Enjoy. Life's too short.*** Keep "tap dancing" to work and owning your space. If you are not enjoying what you do, refocus.
2. ***Know when to take a break.*** Think like a warrior; fight to win. Don't trade for excitement; trade for profits. The market is a very expensive place to look for excitement. When sharp losses are experienced, take time off! The mind can play games following sharp losses. It is not how many times you are right that matters, but how much you make.
3. ***Keep heart and mind healthy.*** Many wizards attribute much of their success to taking the time to think and meditate. Every morning, Amazon CEO Jeff Bezos follows a strict routine that helps him recharge and make

> decisions carefully (see sidebar). Ray Dalio believes that "meditation more than anything in my life was the *biggest* ingredient of whatever success I've had." He writes about using transcendental meditation to reflect on his mistakes and clear his mind in his book *Principles.*

Overcoming the hurdles of your mind—like automatically panicking from plunging stock prices—is the key to following through on the first nine Commandments and long-term success. Practice perception and intuition; mindfulness will allow you to handle stress in the stock market and become a better investor.

If done right—such as following the 10Cs—investing should not be a stressful activity. On the contrary, it should be something you love learning more about, to gain insights and IOT, and conviction. It should be tap dancing. If you find yourself stressed or in a losing streak, slow down, reset, and revisit the 10Cs. If you are enjoying your investing journey, the 10Cs are working. Keep going, profit, and welcome to the world of Wizardry!

Bezos on Slowing Down

Amazon founder Jeff Bezos is the world's richest man, with a net worth of $200 billion as of September 2nd, 2020—more than the GDPs of many countries.[78] We all know that many super successful people like Elon Musk can survive on four hours of sleep a day, or the late Kobe Bryant, who woke up at 4:00 a.m. daily to practice. Bezos also hustled in the early days of Amazon, including doing the packaging himself. Yet, all of them are incredibly mindful of what they are doing.

Jeff Bezos

Today, Bezos is famous for not having the crazy schedule of most business leaders. Instead of heading to the office before sunrise, he stays at home to have breakfast with his kids before heading to work at around 10:00 a.m. Bezos has said, "It takes courage to say, 'Wait. Slow down. Get more information.' Perhaps even ask for help. Begin to unhook from cultural expectations of how to do it, and instead, cultivate the elegant discipline of getting at the deeper truths. Take your business, and your life, into your own hands with a mindfulness practice."

The Ten Commandments in Practice

San, Tim, and Oia have been practicing the 10Cs in their own investing and continue to improve their strategies daily. Here are their stories.

San—Retiree

San is a 51-year-young retiree with three teenage/young adult children in Canada and the US, all enrolled in private schools. San has built a modest "nest egg" from past jobs and investing, and his two keys goals are to grow these assets for both appreciation and dividends to support the family

Self-Assessment

Per **C1: Know Thyself**, San's self-assessment is as follows:

1. **Objectives:**
   a. ***Majority:*** Allocate majority of capital (70%) to safe assets but with sufficient dividends to support family without working full time.
   b. ***Minority:*** Invest material minority of capital (30%) in riskier growth assets to achieve superior, even exceptional, long-term returns.
   c. ***Target returns:*** Target 12% or higher overall average portfolio annual returns over 10 years.
2. **Interests:**
   a. ***Real estate:*** San loves and has invested in real estate, mostly passively in real estate and related assets over decades in China/Asia and North America; he enjoys owning hard assets.

   b. ***Technology:*** An "aspirational geek", San is an early adopter in cool gadgets and tech; he follows them religiously whether it is an Apple device or a Tesla. Beyond tech toys, he is a huge believer in the power of tech to disrupt and to improve human lives.

3. **Style:**
   a. ***Workaholic:*** A self-confessed workaholic who has worked full-time since he immigrated to America at age eight, San post-50 is taking it slightly more easily but still enjoys work/learning.
   b. ***Passive:*** He now prefers to put the majority of his investment (e.g., "work") in primarily passive assets such as rental real estate, for safety and yield.
   c. ***Active:*** San only actively invests in areas he loves and in which he enjoys learning, such as some types of real estate and especially tech disruption opportunities.

4. **Skills:**
   a. ***Master of None:*** A classic Jack of All Trades, Master of None, San has been exposed to numerous industries and markets/geographies from working as a consultant to being a VC/PE investor.
   b. ***Industries:*** He understands real estate and tech well, especially in the China/Asian and North American markets where he has lived/worked most of this life.

5. **Timing:**
   a. Definitely a mid and long-term focused investor
   b. All investments are fundamentally driven

   c. San's real estate investments are three-year-to-eternity plays
   d. Tech picks (e.g., stocks like Tesla) are for long-term fundamentals
   e. Does not understand or enjoy trading or charts
6. **Risks:**
   a. Low risk for "nest egg" passive income (70%)
   b. Mid to high risk for tech/growth bets (30%)
7. **Assets:**
   a. Real estate
   b. Tech/growth companies, assets
8. **Places:**
   a. ***North America***—grew up in New York City, East Coast of the US, lived on the West Coast for a while, now in Toronto so familiar with the North American market, cultures
   b. ***China/Asia***—born in China and lived there 20+ years, also in half a dozen Asian countries so equally fluent and familiar with markets and opportunities in Asia

Applying the 10Cs

Battle Scarred

Unlike Tim and Oia, who are just embarking on their investment journeys, San writes this book at the age of 51 with more battle scars than most. San has violated all the 10Cs many times over and has lost literally tens of millions of his own money and that of clients. Through these lessons, San has also made money along the way and was able to achieve financial independence (FI) before his forties, to take care of his family while living a dream life of traveling the world (55+ countries now—target is 100 before 55). San is happy to share these lessons with Tim, Oia, and readers, and is sure many will achieve FI faster and bigger than San did. San shares his journey through major eras below, and how these lessons and the 10Cs shape his investment strategy today.

Student Days

San was born in China and immigrated to America at age nine, growing up in New York City's Chinatown. San and his three brothers began work early, starting from primary school. They joined their parents at the Chinatown garment factories; San sewed buttons on Jordache jeans after school and weekdays. That was his lunch and book money.

During middle and high school, San worked as a bike messenger, as a busboy and waiter, as a cleaner in a nightclub, and as a bartender. He had a job in telemarketing sales, selling gun licensing services to small businesses. His first entrepreneurial venture was in the 9th grade, blowing $500 saved from odd jobs for a year's wholesale supply of delicious "diet" cookies to help people lose weight. The products never sold and the multi-level marketing firm never accepted the refund, so the cookies piled up in San's cramped bedroom he shared with his three brothers. San swears this is why he remains skinny to this day.

Through college, San also worked various part-time jobs with small businesses to pay his way. Those days were about survival with less cash surplus, but, knowing what he knows now, if he knew then what he knows now, he could have and should have saved a dollar a day from odd jobs to put in a stock or a fund.

C7: Marathon the Winners says that if San had started saving at age nine when he earned his own salary at the garment factories—$1/day or $365/year for the years through, say, college at age 21, compounded at average stock market returns of 7%, his earnings would be worth $147,000 in 2020 (despite only investing a total of $7665). This is why he has set up brokerage accounts for his kids.

Young Professional

After graduating from university, San worked as a management consultant, then as an analyst in a multi-billion-dollar private equity firm. He traveled 75% of the time, and, over 4.5 years, San worked on-site with clients across America and in Canada, Hong Kong, China, Singapore, Indonesia, and Malaysia. On top of salary and bonus, San was given a generous expense account and housing subsidy. A hefty chunk of his income went to Uncle Sam, and the housing allowance went to renting luxury apartments, which he rarely used.

Being single with almost all expenses paid for, San could have easily put away $1000/month to invest (e.g., in equities or tax-deductive investments such as real estate). If, instead, he had used his savings or rent subsidies in 1995 to buy a condo in Hong Kong (where he lived for six years), and kept it to sell today in Hong Kong's cloudy economy, that gain would have been 356%.[79]

Entrepreneur

After 4.5 years as a globe-trotting management consultant, San became smitten by the internet and worked at a Hong Kong dotcom before co-founding oCen, an internet telephony firm, as CFO. He raised $2.5 million of Series A and was soon voted in as CEO. In 2.5 years, he raised over $60 million through seven rounds of venture capital funding with the startup valued at 10 figures, and his stake at nine figures. San hired Lehman Brothers, Bear Stearns, and Piper Jeffries for a dual NASDAQ-Hong Kong IPO. Wealth managers from Goldman to Merrill were also wooing San to manage his soon-to-be-ten-figure wealth, post-IPO.

San had followed eight of the 10 commandments to a tee to early success: he found his calling as a 20-something tech entrepreneur (C1); he found conviction in the future of that sector and the business model—right or wrong (C5); he dedicated 14 to 16 hours days, even spending many nights in the office, definitively surpassing the Magic 10,000 Hours (C5). He was impatient and pushed his team to grow as fast as possible (C6). San even saw the dotcom bubble brewing and was racing against time to get the company listed, so he had sufficient funds to survive before it busted (C3). The bubble did pop, while the company had just started their IPO-round shop. San and his team missed the IPO window by a mere week or two.

The moral of the story from an investing standpoint is not the company's unlucky timing. The lesson is San's failure to follow two of the commandments. San did not diversify—100% of his net worth was tied up in the company's stock. He had no diversification, whatsoever. San had multiple opportunities to sell part of his stake prior to the IPO, and bankers even offered him hedging opportunities in case the risky ventures ran into problems, to diversify. When the bubble did burst and it was "IPO no more," San lost it all.

Never put all your eggs, no matter how golden you feverishly believe it to be, in one basket (C8). Never lose all/lots of money (C9).

Professional Investor

After oCen, San co-founded and co-led a handful more ventures, big and small, with modest success before he was invited to start a China venture capital fund. San had moved to Shanghai in 2002—while of Chinese ethnicity he had grown up in the USA and had dedicated a few years to become fluent in Mandarin, network, and learn the ins/outs of the new China. He also saw the rise of China's economy and opportunities in both consumer and tech, and dedicated time to learn the new space (C1-C5). He was patient to develop the expertise/capabilities he needed (C6) and set out to raise his fund with a modest target of $50 million. Due to the right timing (i.e., rising China—C3, C4) and the prep work, team, etc.—San raised $100 million instead.

San diversified the fund (C8), investing in 16 companies into the portfolio over three years. And, while only a handful were duds (break even, lost money), overall, the portfolio did well (C9), with the fund being named in the Top 30/Top 50 by influential industry publications.

The main mistake, in retrospect, was the fund structure. Unlike Kathy Xu's fund, or Berkshire Hathaway, San's fund was a typical "GP/LP" structure with a seven-to-10-year life, which meant the fund had to return money to investors. The fund was thus forced to sell all the winners, including winners that made it to public markets and were still growing fast, and pre-IPO winners at 2 to 3x which, if here were still holding them, could have brought in much higher returns.

So, going into today, San has all 10Cs in mind.

Today

San's key investment objective at age 51 is developing an "all weather, high-yield" portfolio that requires only part-time work while providing safety and cash flows for living expenses and retirement. The 10Cs guide him daily on his 60/30/10 portfolio:

1. ***60%:*** safe, high-yield long-term passive assets, primarily real estate debt and equity
   a. ***Debt:*** Canadian mortgage funds yielding 8.5% or higher (one to three months' liquidity)
   b. ***Housing:*** US workforce housing, particularly B and C grade multi-family apartment buildings yielding 8% to 10% quarterly and 1.5-2.0x returns (over three to seven years)
   c. ***Other:*** safe, long-term real-estate investments such as farmland, self-storage, and mobile home parks (three-to-10-year holds)
2. ***30%:*** growth stocks and diversification funds/ETFs
   a. ***Religion Stocks:*** San has a handful of growth stocks he "marathons" as long-term winners. His favorite is Tesla, which he follows with religious fervor and equally religious conviction. Other top stocks are Tencent, Alibaba, Apple, and India's JIO (Reliance).

b. ***Diversification:*** To achieve diversification, San buys into market or industry ETFs, or funds that help diversify into wider industries or markets.

3. ***10%:*** as a former venture capitalist, San is comfortable with risking no more than 10% of capital into moonshots that can be 100x plays (or bust)

a. ***Tech:*** Other than his above "religion stocks," which are established public companies, San advises for equity and occasionally invests in startups that may turn into established public companies one day. For example, he recently invested in an insect protein venture.

b. ***Other:*** A small percentage is invested in the risky "other" category, such as Bitcoin and crypto currencies, for further diversification.

San's current portfolio is constructed following the 10Cs strictly. This includes having clear objectives, then investing in assets he has passion for and that he understands. He prioritizes doing the homework and gaining conviction before investing, achieving uncorrelated asset types and geographic diversification, and investing in the long term, rather than trading.

Tim—Young Professional

Tim is a 22-year-old young adult/professional who considers himself fortunate to have graduated from college without student debt. His main goal in his twenties is to grow his asset base to achieve financial independence. He believes that everyone will benefit from a good financial education, especially parents who want to start educating their children early to take advantage of the magic of compounding!

Self-Assessment

1. **Objectives:**
    a. ***Majority:*** Allocate 80% of portfolio for buying and holding medium-risk investments
    b. ***Minority:*** Allocate 20% of portfolio for short-term, high-conviction trading ideas
    c. ***Target Return:*** Target seven to 10% annual portfolio growth, the more the better :)
    d. ***Growing Asset Base:*** Invest in his stock portfolio and perhaps learn real estate investing
2. **Interests:**
    a. ***Technology:*** He likes being young, trendy, and tech savvy (who doesn't?).

   b. ***Renewable Energy:*** He likes geography and physics, and believes global warming is real.
   c. ***Financial Services:*** He likes learning about new fin-tech that are disrupting the consumer finance space.
3. **Style:**
   a. ***Compounding:*** Hopefully he has at least 60 more years to live, so time will do the work.
   b. ***Passive to Active:*** Start with 50% in passive investments and shift to more active model with time and more experience.
4. **Skills:**
   a. ***Tech-Savvy:*** Love learning about user interface design, technology specs, and competitive implications
   b. ***Historian:*** Loves to read biographies, and about historical developments. Likes getting a macro and critical view of world developments
   c. ***Valuation:*** Good grasp on basic valuation, though there's much to learn
   d. ***Zen:*** Not easily fazed emotionally, constantly reminding himself to stay objective and not invest out of impulse
5. **Timing:**
   a. Investment horizon of at least three years and ideally five-plus years
   b. occasionally shorting companies that he deems overheated (<20% of portfolio total)
6. **Risks:**
   a. low risk for long-term holding passive equity index funds (30%)

   b. medium risk for technology and REITs investments (60%) and commodities (10%)
7. **Assets:**
   a. equities, REITs, and commodities
8. **Places:**
   a. North America—familiar with the culture and market of that part of the world
   b. China/Asia—grew up in Hong Kong and regularly visited China; knows how quickly China has developed and excited for its prospects in the long term

Applying the 10Cs

San's battle scars are certainly impressive, but Tim also has some battle scars (well, maybe bruises relative to San's scars) of his own too.

Compounding (C7) from Childhood

Growing up in Hong Kong, Tim always considered Chinese New Year the second-best holiday of the year (after Mid-Autumn Festival with the beautiful lanterns and tasty mooncakes). Aunts and uncles will give kids red envelopes sealed with cold-hard cash, usually $5 to $25, depending on how generous they are, and his grandparents would always be the most generous of all, giving $50 to each of their grandchildren. Visiting with family or friend-to-friend, Tim would be able to amass a fortune ($400 on average) each year! But this was not pocket money that Tim could spend at will.

Starting from a young age, Tim learned from his parents the power of compounding. Even though he barely grasped the miracle of the concept, he would "volunteer" to have his parents invest his money in passive index funds and keep $10 to himself, enough to buy a pack of bubble gum, a few bags of chips, and a bottle of coke. Watching his friends splurging their red envelope money at the snack shop, Tim inevitably felt a little scarred on the inside (he's being a little dramatic, we know).

Market Cycles (C3/C4) from 2008 Global Financial Crisis

Tim remembers 2008: he was as clueless as any other fourth grader in the classroom. He continued to invest in his account with his red envelope money; the principal invested over the years had more than doubled—all without Tim doing anything. Then suddenly, one day in 2009, Tim's parents showed him the balance in his investment account—the portfolio had lost 40% of its value. Nearly all his gains were wiped out, and it was his first encounter with the big downturn in the long-term market cycles. Again, Tim inevitably felt a little scarred by the number of McDonald's ice cream cones he had lost within a year.

Learning (C1/C2) from Simulation and Researching

Entering high school, Tim watched the markets long enough that he wanted to try his hand at active investing. Tim really did not know many companies, so he put 20% of his portfolio in each of the companies he knew from life: Apple, Tencent, Microsoft, Nintendo, and BMW. The only bad investment was Nintendo, which released the disappointing Wii U gaming console, causing the stock price to stay flat. Due to the recovering economy, Tim was lucky to have everything else in his portfolio do well.

About eight years ago, his parents and some relatives started discussing financial literacy for the younger generation and came up with the idea of compiling a "Bible" summarizing the philosophies of famous investors and traders. So, 14-year-old Tim proceeded over the following years to help research and write investor profiles for the book. Tim had since read many investment books (like *The Warren Buffett Way* and *One Up On Wall Street)* and gradually learned the basics from the investment greats. No scars here!

Bulldozed by Risk (C8/C9) from His First Ventures

The biggest lessons are the ones that hurt you the most. At one point, Tim's portfolio was down a whopping 50%.

Tim started his active investing career as a speculator, not an investor. When he first opened his stock brokerage account to invest (read: trade and speculate), he found the stock market an intriguing place. In the first month, his "superior" stock-picking skills landed him a 5% gain (on an up market). The next month, he lost 2% while the market was flat. Two months in, he was already feeling uneasy and impatient, and wanted to find ways to grow his portfolio faster. This led him to leveraged gold miners ETF.

Tim knew nothing about gold at this time (or anything, really). He knew nothing of the relationship between gold, dollar strength, and interest rates (probably the most basic knowledge any gold speculator should have), and knew only that miner indexes like NUGT and DUST returned three times the daily return of the normal miner index—great place to be for an amateur speculator confident of his market timing acumens. Winning some and losing even more, Tim upped the weighting of the miners ETFs with time, starting from 10% to eventually 70% of his portfolio, hoping to win back increasing losses, which kept piling up. After four months of speculating between classes, Tim managed to wipe out 30% of his portfolio (50% at one point) and was ready to call it quits. Tim has finally learned the need to stop speculating, learn fundamental analysis, and invest for the long term.

Keep Learning (C5/C6/C10) from Experienced Professionals

After taking a few months off to mind his mind, Tim started investing again with a long-term view. Between managing his portfolio and his professional experience working with three different investment funds in Hong Kong and New York, Tim was learning to seek religion on his investments.

In his first job, Tim spent the summer shadowing the CIO of a top performing HK/China hedge fund. Tim studied primarily Chinese investments (including the famous BAT technology Trio – Baidu, Alibaba, and Tencent), summarized management earning calls with analysts and shareholders, and drafted investment reports and updates for the CIO and fund managers.

For his year-long second job (full-time summer, part-time sophomore year at Columbia), Tim worked for the CIO of a New York-based family office, investing in other actively managed hedge funds, as well as managing its own direct stock portfolio investments in the US. From the myriad of hedge funds that pitched to the family office seeking investments, Tim was exposed to a variety of investment strategies adopted by the various funds to gain advantages over the market and competition. Tim also learned to analyze and make recommendations of US stocks for the family office's own portfolio, primarily of high-conviction ideas from fund managers working with the family office.

In the third fund, Tim worked in a US-based hedge fund focusing on technology/consumer companies in the greater Asia region. This time, Tim gained further insights, and delved deeply into quantitative analysis and valuation methodologies, building detailed financial models to supplement the qualitative analysis performed in order to gain a comprehensive understanding of investment merits of target opportunities.

Tim gradually developed an increasingly deeper understanding of investing and the markets. Over the past five years, Tim has continued to see his portfolio fluctuate, but managed to generate an average of 8% return a year, recouping the money lost through his speculative "younger days" and making a handsome amount on top of that. Upon graduating from Columbia in 2021, Tim will work as a management consultant to gain insights on the decision-making processes of business leaders at the strategic and operational levels, which will no doubt help Tim to even better assess merits and risks of future investment opportunities.

Knowing what he knows today, Tim will apply the 10Cs in the following ways:

1. **C1: Know Thyself:** Stay invested in equities and real estate. Tim does not want 0% growth on his hard-earned income.
2. **C2: Own Your Space:** Stick to technology and consumer retail plays, primarily in the US and China

3. **C3: Respect Market Cycles:** Refrain from short-term speculations and instead focus on the longer term economic and market cycles; invest with at least a one-year time horizon.
4. **C4: Don't Be a Dead Fish:** Keep an independent mind. Don't invest in something simply because of some "talking heads" or a Seeking Alpha article recommending it. Look out for favorable risk/reward opportunities to surface from overshot situations resulting from greed and fear.
5. **C5: Seek Religion:** Put money to potential investments only after thorough homework has been done. Gain better understanding of financial accounting to get a more accurate read of the financial health of companies, and to potentially avoid investing in fraudulent ones.
6. **C6: Be Patient, Be Bold:** Do **C5: Seek Religion** properly, and this will not be a problem
7. **C7: Marathon the Winners:** Keep putting money in early and consistently. Using time to build longer term wealth is a hundred times more effective than anything else out there.
8. **C8 Diversify...Just Enough:** Half of the portfolio in passive index funds, eight to 10 investments for the other half.
9. **C9: Don't Lose Money:** Zero leverage. Have a game plan and never put more than 10% of your portfolio into any single investment.

10. **C10: Mind the Mind:** Be humble, unemotional, and forward-looking. Refrain from being carried away by past wins or losses.

Oia—Student

Oia is a 17-year-old student who lives in Toronto, Canada. She is a senior at a boarding high school in New Hampshire and learns about the 10Cs in her spare time with the intention of achieving financial independence by her twenties. She wants to be able to pursue her passions, including social entrepreneurship and traveling, without financial constraints or reliance on her parents.

Self-Assessment

1. **Objectives:**
   a. ***Majority:*** allocate 70% of capital to invest in the stock market, utilizing the buy and hold strategy

   b. ***Minority:*** continue to learn and help close at least two passive income generative properties by the end of 2021
   c. ***Target Return:*** target 12% or higher annual portfolio growth
2. **Interests:**
   a. ***Stock market:*** learn market basics by diving into stocks
      i. Calculate intrinsic value and picking investments with confidence and without outside influence
      ii. Choose four to seven stocks to consistently research and keep up with
   c. ***Real estate:*** passive income generative multifamily real estate investment in the US and abroad
      i. Continue to practice underwriting and financial analysis
      ii. Conduct analysis on markets all over the world
      iii. Familiarize herself with the legal processes of closing a deal
3. **Style:**
   a. ***Passive:*** invest majority of capital early and boldly in the stock market
   b. ***Active:*** use above passive income and US loan structure to help close properties, funneling 100% returns back into co-investing in new properties part-time during college
4. **Skills:**
   a. ***Detail-oriented:*** diligent perfectionist with strong analytical writing skills

   b. ***Motivated:*** high-powered work ethic stemming from passion for investment and financial independence
   c. ***Multicultural:*** open-minded to all types of people, cultures, and yearning for constant learning
5. **Timing**:
   a. ***Long-term, fundamental:*** especially as a busy student, letting time do the work, holding and compounding
6. **Risks:**
   a. *Mid-high* risk for technology investments
7. **Assets:**
   a. ***Real estate:*** help close and co-own passive-income generative multifamily residences
   b. ***Stocks:*** as of today, majority technology companies
8. **Places:**
   a. ***China/Asia***—grew up in Shanghai and Taipei, fluent in Mandarin and Korean as well as respective cultures
   b. ***North America***—currently living in Toronto, frequenting New Hampshire, Maryland, and New York

Applying the 10Cs

I got my first taste of technology addiction at age four, when my parents gifted my sisters and me iPod Touches for Christmas. I quickly became an expert on all things Apple, learning to download Taylor Swift songs from the iTunes Store and mastering the art of DoodleJump. If I had invested $40 (a portion of my Chinese New Year red envelope money) in Apple that year, my

$40 would be worth $767 today, roughly a 2000% return. Of course, no one expects a four year-old to spend their New Year's money on Apple stock rather than App Store games or popsicles from the corner store.

What is important is that whether it is in a S&P 500 index fund, savings account, or the real estate market, time, not money, is the commodity. American investor and author of Rich Dad Poor Dad Robert Kiyosaki offered the distinction that "the only difference between a rich person and poor person is how they use their time".

Having understood the importance of investing early, I began to look for ways to get investment capital and produce income without relying on my parents.

In April 2020, I started to think seriously about investing in the stock market. As COVID-19 fears heightened and the markets sold off sharply, I knew I wanted to "be greedy when others are fearful" (C4).

As I watched the market plummet day after day, I was tempted to listen to experts (Buffett, who believed that the crash had not come) and self-proclaimed experts (young investors on YouTube and TikTok were rampant, offering advice left and right). After realizing that no one could predict the bottom, I began to settle on my own strategy (C1).

I decided to be a long-term investor, and I believed that the stocks on my watchlist, especially the resilient tech ones, were undervalued or could at least hold their value (C5). I used cash saved up from jobs to buy shares of Microsoft, Tencent, and Tesla (C8), all companies I had extensively researched and regularly kept up with (C5).

While the market fluctuated in the next weeks, I fought against urges to sell (C10), reminding myself of my long-term strategy and conviction in the companies (C7). Months later, I made additional small purchases in the same companies and reinvested dividends, but largely kept my portfolio the same and held the same conviction in my stocks. In return, my portfolio has yielded a 38% return so far. While this is an unusual year with unusual returns, I will continue to use this strategy in the coming years.

To supplement my passive income from my stock portfolio, I want to focus on the more active, low risk high payoff multi-family real estate sector. I am studying the BRRR (Buy, Rehab, Rent, Refinance) strategy, becoming comfortable with identifying a good potential buy and running through a full financial model, including market analysis, rehabilitation process, the American loan structure, and property sale.

By looking at sample deals, I try to understand financial models so that I can differentiate between a good and bad deal. I hope to own more and more of the space as I learn more of the real estate sector and help in researching and closing deals; I wish to eventually co-invest in a property.

Goals

Through my sources of passive and active income, my ultimate goal is to become financially literate and achieve financial independence. I want to become free of restrictive time and financial burdens.

Portfolio Strategy

1. Invest all capital in the stock market, will not let it sit in a low-interest savings account.

2. Invest long-term and fundamentally; hold onto winners through ups and downs. Primarily focus on technology for recession-proofing and index funds for low risk diversification.
3. Learn to determine intrinsic value, run financial analysis, and research consistently before investing in a stock, rather than making decisions influenced by experts or family members. Limit to four to seven investments that I can commit to keeping up with as a full-time student.

DIY Self-Assessment

Category	Self-Reflection
Objectives	• •
Interests	• •
Styles	• •
Skills	• •

Timing	•
Risks	•
Assets	•
Places	•

CALL TO ACTION

"Until it's on paper, it's vapor."
Sir John Hargrove

Hargrove wrote the book *Mind Hacking,* which proposes we write down our resolutions and condition our minds positively and meaningfully. He shared the story of the actor and comedian Jim Carey, and how he exercised this approach to a tee.

While Carrey was a struggling actor, fully unemployed, he wrote himself a $10 million check and put "Acting Services Rendered" in the detail line. He dated it 10 years into the future and kept it in his wallet so he could see the $10 million check daily. Ten year later, Carrey was cast in the movie "Dumb and Dumber." The contract? $10 million dollars.

Visualize whatever you want in life—what things you want, what you want to do, what you want to learn, and whom you want to help—and write them down, both in and outside of the realm of investment. Many successful businesspeople and investors we know like to Google the beach house they want to live in, or the yacht they want to own. They print it out in full color and pasted it on their walls, office desks, or refrigerators to remind themselves that this is theirs, at a future date they have clearly defined. They then work hard to get it and are reminded daily of those beautiful images.

Next, put weight on these goals—use emotional, powerful words and write down why you *must* achieve them. Infuse elements of your goals everywhere in your life, putting up photos of the car you want or even writing yourself a check like Carrey for your future investment earnings. This type of manifestation and law of attraction may seem silly at first, but we strongly believe they alter and orient your mindset towards your desires.

Lastly, remember to stay humble in the midst of successes, no matter how big they become. A psychology of arrogance and overconfidence is what allows you to lose big. Continue learning ceaselessly—one place you can do that is on our companion website, free since you purchased this book. In our community of like-minded Wizards students, you can continuously learn and network with other investors of all experience and backgrounds.

Let's take action. *Carpe diem!*

GLOSSARY

Alternative asset classes: any other asset classes excluding stocks, bonds, or cash

Arbitrage: the simultaneous buying or selling of similar and highly correlated assets in different markets to take advantage of difference in pricing for the same product

Asset-Under-Management (AUM): value of financial assets that a financial institution (banks/funds) manages

Asymmetric loss profile: achieving more positive gains than negatives with active risk management

Bonds: a security that demonstrates the indebtedness of the bond issuer to the bold holders. A bond can be issued by the government, organizations, or a person.

Blue chip companies: typically a well-established company with a good reputation and sound financials

Brokerage house: the company that finds buyers or sellers to help you trade your investments

Bulls and Bears: the animal spirits. Bulls represent an up market. Bears represent a down market.

Chief Investment Officer (CIO): the most senior executive in charge of the company's investments

Collateral: a valuable asset used to secure a loan. Lenders can seize the asset if the borrower fails to make payment on their loan.

Derivatives: a financial asset whose value is based on the value of another financial asset

Distressed fund: an investment fund that specializes in buying companies experiencing financial stress

Exchange-Traded Fund (ETF): works like a mutual fund, except you can go in and out of the fund much quicker as they can be freely bought and sold during regular stock market hours

Hedge fund: an investment fund that trades relatively liquid assets and uses more complex trading and portfolio techniques to pursue higher-than-market returns

Initial Public Offering (IPO): the process of a company issuing shares to the public to raise capital through a stock exchange listing

Individual Retirement Account (IRA): a tax-advantaged investment vehicle that gives you tax benefits

Insider trading: illegal trades made based on non-public (insider) information

Limit order: an order that will not be executed unless it hits the specified price

Mean: represents the average number in mathematics

Nominal return: the nominal impact return without considering inflation

PE Ratio: Price / Earnings. The higher the ratio, the more inflated (expensive) the valuation is.

Real Estate Investment Trust (REITs): companies that own and manage real estate assets. REITs give investors a liquid and easy exposure to real estate investments through the stock market.

Real return: the actual return you get after accounting for (deducting) inflation out of the nominal return

Recession: a part of the business cycle where the economy contracts and experiences a decline in economic activity

Short: the opposite of longing/buying a stock. When you short a stock, you profit when the price goes down, as you can buy it in the future at a lower price.

Stock: shares representing ownership in a company. If the company has 100 shares, owning one share will give you 1% (1/100) ownership of the company.

Stock market index: an index representing share price of a basket of stocks. Examples include the S&P 500 Index (around 500 of the biggest companies in the US), NASDAQ index (stock exchange for major technology companies), and the Hong Kong Hang Seng Index.

Subprime: prime means optimal. So, subprime describes less-than-optimal, lower quality, and more risky investments.

Super platforms: scalable applications or web-based services that have a loyal user base and good expansion/growth potential

Technical signals: the share price patterns formed by analyzing historical price and volume data

Treasury bond: government debt securities issued by the US federal government. Investors buying bonds lend money to the government and get "interest payments" in return.

Bibliography

Amadeo, Kimberly. "How a 1998 Bailout Led to the 2008 Financial Crisis." *The Balance,* 2020, www.thebalance.com/long-term-capital-crisis-3306240.

Bar Eli, Michael, et al. "Action Bias Among Elite Soccer Goalkeepers: The Case of Penalty Kicks." SSRN, February 9, 2008, papers.ssrn.com/sol3/papers.cfm?abstract_id=1091662.

Browne, Christopher H. *The Little Book of Value Investing.* Wiley, 2010.

Cassidy, John. "Mastering the Machine." *The New Yorker*, 2011.

Dudley, Chris. "Money Lessons Learned from Pro Athletes' Financial Fouls." CNBC, May 15, 2018, www.cnbc.com/2018/05/14/money-lessons-learned-from-pro-athletes-financial-fouls.html.

Eng, San. "Kathy Xu: China's Queen of Venture Capital." Wizards Institute, 2020. https://www.youtube.com/watch?v=VeHP-3b0ccFM&ab_channel=WizardsInstitute

Farah, Lynn. "Mukesh vs Anil: How the Ambani Brothers' Wealth Soared and Dipped." *South China Morning Post*, July 20, 2020.

Fifield, Aaron. "Knowing Your Edge—Surviving the Game | Blair Hull." Season 1, episode 85, 2016.

Franck, Tom. "Warren Buffett Says Berkshire Sold All Its Airline Stocks because of the Coronavirus." CNBC, May 4, 2020.

Gabler, Neal. "The Secret Shame of Middle-Class Americans Living Paycheck to Paycheck." *The Atlantic*, July 11, 2018.

GDP per Capita. Worldometer, 2017, https://www.worldometers.info/gdp/gdp-per-capita/

Graham, Benjamin. The Intelligent Investor. *Harper,* 2006.

Guo, X. (2008). The fall of long-term capital management. Lingnan Journal of Banking, Finance and Economics, 1. Retrieved from http://commons.ln.edu.hk/ljbfe/vol1/iss1/1

Hoffower, Hillary. "Warren Buffett Has Lost More than $21 Billion in the First Months of 2020. Here's How the Notoriously Frugal Billionaire Spends His $67.6 Billion Fortune."

Business Insider, March 23, 2020, www.businessinsider.com/how-warren-buffett-spends-net-worth-philanthropy-2018-10.

Kahneman, D., and A. Deaton. "High Income Improves Evaluation of Life but Not Emotional Well-Being." *Proceedings of the National Academy of Sciences*, vol. 107, no. 38, 2010, pp. 16489–16493., doi:10.1073/pnas.1011492107.

Kaufman, Josh. *The First 20 Hours: How to Learn Anything... Fast.* Portfolio/Penguin, 2014.

Lattman, Peter. "Treasure Hunters of the Financial Crisis." *The New York Times,* November 9 2013, www.nytimes.com/2013/11/10/business/treasure-hunters-of-the-financial-crisis.html.

Marks, Howard. *Mastering the Market Cycle: Getting the Odds on Your Side.* Nicholas Brealey Publishing, 2020.

Marks, Howard. "Yet Again?" Oaktree Capital, 2017.

Palmer, Annie. "Jeff Bezos Is Now Worth More than $200 Billion." CNBC, August 26, 2020, www.cnbc.com/2020/08/26/amazon-ceo-jeff-bezos-worth-more-than-200-billion.html.

Politi, James, and Colby Smith. "Fed Inflation Shift Raises Questions about Past Rate Rises." *Financial Times,* August 28, 2020, www.ft.com/content/e1a3a865-1738-40b3-9180-2ca8f886f4f0.

Quantitative Analysis of Investor Behavior. Dalbar, 2017.

Ritholtz, Barry. "Six Rules of Michael Steinhardt." *The Big Picture*, February 28, 2012, ritholtz.com/2010/09/six-rules-of-michael-steinhardt/.

Schwager, Jack D. "Diversification: Why 10 Is Not Enough." *Market Sense and Nonsense: How the Markets Really Work (and How They Don't)*. Wiley, 2013.

Sengupta, Devina. "Reliance Jio Plans to Capture over 50% of Revenue Market - ET Telecom." ETTelecom.com, March 3, 2017.

Sharpe, William F. "Likely Gains from Market Timing." *Financial Analysts Journal*, vol. 31, no. 2, 1975, pp. 60–69., doi:10.2469/faj.v31.n2.60.

Singh, Manish. "Reliance Jio Platforms Says $15.2 Billion Fund-raise Is Good for Now." *TechCrunch*, June 19, 2020.

The S&P 500 P/E Ratio: A Historical Perspective. ValueScope. https://www.valuescopeinc.com/wp-content/uploads/2017/07/White-Papers-SP-500-PE-Ratio.pdf

Sweeney, Chris. "Hugh Hendry: Wit and Wisdom of Ex-Financier Turned YouTube Star." Scotland | *The Times,* September 7, 2020.

Torngren, Gustaf, and Montgomery, Henry. "Worse Than Chance? Performance and Confidence Among Professionals and Laypeople in the Stock Market." *Journal of Behavioral*

Finance, vol. 5, no. 3, 2004, pp. 148–153., doi:10.1207/s15427579jpfm0503_3.

Twenge, Jean M., and A. Bell Cooper. "The Expanding Class Divide in Happiness in the United States, 1972–2016." *Emotion*, 2020, doi:10.1037/emo0000774.

Winn, Howard. "Anthony Bolton Retires with Unfond Memories of China." April 2, 2014, www.scmp.com/business/article/1463349/anthony-bolton-retires-unfond-memories-china.

About the Authors

San Eng: An "investorpreneur," San has founded and led half a dozen companies, raising $150 million in venture capital as an entrepreneur and deploying $500 million in capital as a professional investor. San's private equity firm has been ranked in the Top 30 in China amongst thousands of funds. San has invested across technology, consumer, telecom, utilities, infrastructure, education, healthcare, blockchain, agrifoods, real estate, and other asset classes in Asia and North America. He is most proud that his investments have created thousands of jobs.

San kickstarted the book project, helping to set the general direction, and applying learnings from decades of investing experience mixed with extensive research and direct interactions (investing and interviews) with hundreds of Wizards.

Tim Eng: Tim's investment journey started in high school, when he started to read dozens of investment books, helped create dozens of Wizards profiles for this book, and began to invest and trade using paper and then real money portfolios. Tim now has eight years of investment experience and hopes to continue to improve on his average 8%+ annual returns. Moreover, Tim spent three summers working at investment funds focused on the US, Hong Kong, and the rest of Asia. Tim is a senior studying Computer Science and History at Columbia University.

Tim is the main voice of the book, applying his passion for both writing and investing (including trading and speculating) to years of his own comprehensive investment research to make *Ten Commandments of Investing* a cogent, coherent book.

Oia Eng: A high school senior at Phillips Exeter Academy, Oia grew up in Shanghai, Taipei, New Hampshire, and Toronto. She took an early interest in the F.I.R.E (Financial Independence, Retire Early) movement after reading Robert Kiyosaki's *Rich Dad, Poor Dad* and Tim Ferriss' *4-Hour Work Week.* After working long hours as a waitress, tutor, and at other odd jobs, Oia realizes that her time is her most precious commodity. She is growing her passive income streams in order to achieve financial independence early in life so she can pursue her passions without limits. Oia wrote several core chapters of the *Ten Commandments* as well as led research efforts; she also helped drive the structure and tone of the book, striking the right balance between quality content and ease of learning for the reader.

ABOUT THE ILLUSTRATOR

Special mention and thank you to Chloe Eng, Oia's younger sister, who drew all the Investment Wizards. Chloe chose red for each Wizard, a color symbolizing wealth and prosperity in many cultures. For her cover design, she chose the color green, which in many cultures is a symbol of wealth and prosperity.

Endnotes

1 Alternative asset classes: any other asset classes excluding stocks, bonds, or cash

2 Hedge fund: an investment fund that trades relatively-liquid assets and uses more complex trading and portfolio techniques to pursue higher-than-market returns.

3 Gabler, Neal. "The Secret Shame of Middle-Class Americans Living Paycheck to Paycheck." *The Atlantic*, July 11, 2018.

4 Stocks: shares representing ownership in a company. If the company has 100 shares, owning one share will give you 1% (1/100) ownership of the company.

5 Politi, James, and Colby Smith, "Fed Inflation Shift Raises Questions about Past Rate Rises," *Financial Times*, August 28, 2020, www.ft.com/content/e1a3a865-1738-40b3-9180-2ca8f886f4f0. (accessed Sept 10, 2020)

6 Treasury bond: government debt securities issued by the US federal government. Investors buying bonds lend money to the government and get "interest payments" in return.

7 Nominal return: the nominal return without considering inflation.

8 Real return: the actual return you get after accounting for (deducting) inflation out of the nominal return.

9 Twenge, Jean M., and A. Bell Cooper, "The Expanding Class Divide in Happiness in the United States, 1972–2016," *Emotion*, 2020, doi:10.1037/emo0000774.

10 Kahneman, D., and A. Deaton. "High Income Improves Evaluation of Life but Not Emotional Well-Being." *Proceedings of the National Academy of Sciences*, vol. 107, no. 38, 2010, pp. 16489–16493., doi:10.1073/pnas.1011492107.

11 Data from: GDP per Capita, Worldometer, 2017, https://www.worldometers.info/gdp/gdp-per-capita/. (accessed Sept 24, 2020)

12 Hoffower, Hillary. "Warren Buffett Has Lost More than $21 Billion in the First Months of 2020. Here's How the Notoriously Frugal Billionaire Spends His $67.6 Billion Fortune." *Business Insider*, March 23, 2020, www.businessinsider.com/how-warren-buffett-spends-net-worth-philanthropy-2018-10. (accessed Sept 08, 2020)

13 Ritholtz, Barry. "Six Rules of Michael Steinhardt." *The Big Picture*, February 28, 2012, ritholtz.com/2010/09/six-rules-of-michael-steinhardt/. (accessed May 10, 2020)

14 Chris Dudley, senior wealth advisor and director of sports and entertainment at Boston Private Wealth. "Money Lessons Learned from Pro Athletes' Financial Fouls." CNBC, May 15, 2018, www.cnbc.com/2018/05/14/mon-

ey-lessons-learned-from-pro-athletes-financial-fouls.html. (accessed Sept 10, 2020)

15 Assets Under Management: value of financial assets that a financial institution (banks/funds) controls.

16 Brokerage house: a company that finds buyers or sellers to help you trade your investments.

17 REITs: companies that own and operate real estate. REITs give investors a more liquid and management-free way of getting exposure to real estate investments.

18 Bonds: a type of security that demonstrates the indebtedness of the bond issuer to the bold holders. A bond can be issued by the government, organizations, or a person.

19 Kaufman, Josh. The First 20 Hours: How to Learn Anything...Fast. NY, NY: Portfolio/Penguin, 2014.

20 Stock market index: a number to track the market performance of a combination of selected stocks. Examples include the S&P 500 Index (around 500 of the biggest companies in the US), NASDAQ index (stock exchange for major technology companies), and the Hong Kong Hang Seng Index.

21 Initial Public Offering (IPO): the process of a company issuing shares to the public to raise capital.

22 Bulls and Bears: bulls represent an up market. Bears represent a down market.

23 Short: the opposite of longing/buying a stock. When you short a stock, you profit when the price goes down, as you can buy it later at a lower price.

24 Tesla analyst Dan Ives of Wedbush Markets interview at https://wizards.institute/

25 Subprime: prime means optimal. So subprime describes less-than-optimal, untrustworthy investments.

26 Recession: a part of the business cycle where the economy contracts and experiences a decline in economic activity.

27 Marks, Howard. *Mastering the Market Cycle: Getting the Odds on Your Side*. London: Nicholas Brealey Publishing, 2020.

28 Marks, Howard. "Yet Again?" Oaktree Capital, 2017.

29 Distressed Fund: an investment fund that specializes in buying companies experiencing financial stress.

30 Lattman, Peter. "Treasure Hunters of the Financial Crisis." *The New York Times*, November 9, 2013, www.nytimes.com/2013/11/10/business/treasure-hunters-of-the-financial-crisis.html.

31 Data from: The S&P 500 P/E Ratio: A Historical Perspective. ValueScope. https://www.valuescopeinc.com/wp-content/uploads/2017/07/White-Papers-SP-500-PE-Ratio.pdf

32 PE Ratio: Price / Earnings. The higher the ratio, the more inflated (expensive) the valuation is.

33 Sharpe, William F. "Likely Gains from Market Timing." *Financial Analysts Journal*, vol. 31, no. 2, 1975, pp. 60–69., doi:10.2469/faj.v31.n2.60.

34 Insider trading: illegal trades made based on non-public (insider) information.

35 Technical signals: the patterns found by analyzing historical price and volume

36 Fifield, Aaron. "Knowing Your Edge—Surviving the Game | Blair Hull." Season 1, episode 85, 2016.

37 Ibid.

38 Exchange-Traded Fund: works like a mutual fund, except you can go in and out of the fund much more quickly, as they can be freely bought and sold during regular stock market hours.

39 Torngren, Gustaf, and Montgomery, Henry. "Worse Than Chance? Performance and Confidence Among Professionals and Laypeople in the Stock Market." *Journal of Behavioral Finance*, vol. 5, no. 3, 2004, pp. 148–153., doi:10.1207/s15427579jpfm0503_3.

40 Blue chip companies: Typically well-established companies with a good reputation and sound financials

41 Torngren and Montgomery. "Worse Than Chance."

42 Ibid.

43 Ibid.

44 Chief Investment Officer (CIO): job title of the most senior executive in charge of the company's investments.

45 Sweeney, Chris. "Hugh Hendry: Wit and Wisdom of Ex-Financier Turned YouTube Star." *Scotland | The Times*, September 7, 2020.

46 Asymmetric loss profile. achieving more positive gains than negatives with active risk management.

47 Graham, Benjamin. The Intelligent Investor. Harper, 2006.

48 Mean: represents the average number in mathematics.

49 Data from: Quantitative Analysis of Investor Behavior. Dalbar, 2017.

50 Ibid.

51 Super platforms: Scalable applications or web-based services that have a loyal user base and high growth.

52 Eng, San. "Kathy Xu: China's Queen of Venture Capital." Wizards Institute, 2020. https://www.youtube.com/watch?v=VeHP3b0ccFM&ab_channel=WizardsInstitute
53 Winn, Howard. "Anthony Bolton Retires with Unfond Memories of China." *South China Morning Post*, April 2, 2014, www.scmp.com/business/article/1463349/anthony-bolton-retires-unfond-memories-china.
54 Browne, Christopher H. *The Little Book of Value Investing*. Hoboken, NJ: Wiley, 2007.
55 Collateral: a valuable asset used to secure a loan. Lenders can seize the asset if the borrower fails to make payment on their loan.
56 Bar Eli, Michael, et al. "Action Bias Among Elite Soccer Goalkeepers: The Case of Penalty Kicks." SSRN, February 9, 2008, papers.ssrn.com/sol3/papers.cfm?abstract_id=1091662.
57 Ibid.
58 Singh, Manish. "Reliance Jio Platforms Says $15.2 Billion Fundraise Is Good for Now." TechCrunch, June 19, 2020.
59 Sengupta, Devina. "Reliance Jio Plans to Capture over 50% of Revenue Market - ET Telecom." ETTelecom.com, March 3, 2017.
60 Farah, Lynn. "Mukesh vs Anil: How the Ambani Brothers' Wealth Soared and Dipped." *South China Morning Post*, July 20, 2020.
61 Ritholtz. "Six Rules of Michael Steinhardt."
62 Inman, Phillip. "Black Wednesday 20 Years On: How the Day Unfolded." *The Guardian*, Guardian News and

Media, September 13, 2012, www.theguardian.com/business/2012/sep/13/black-wednesday-20-years-pound-erm.
63 Eng. "Kathy Xu: China's Queen of Venture Capital."
64 Individual Retirement Account: a tax-advantaged investment vehicle that gives you tax benefits.
65 Cassidy, John. "Mastering the Machine." *The New Yorker*, 2011.
66 Schwager, Jack D. *Market Sense and Nonsense: How the Markets Really Work (and How They Don't)*. Hoboken, NJ: Wiley, 2013, pp. 267–275.
67 Franck, Tom. "Warren Buffett Says Berkshire Sold All Its Airline Stocks because of the Coronavirus." CNBC, May 4, 2020.
68 Limit order: an order that will not be executed unless it hits the specified price.
69 Leverage: the use of borrowed money in investing to amplify profits (or loss).
70 Amadeo, Kimberly. "How a 1998 Bailout Led to the 2008 Financial Crisis." *The Balance*, 2020, www.thebalance.com/long-term-capital-crisis-3306240.
71 Derivatives: a financial asset whose value is based on the value of another financial asset
72 Ibid.
73 Arbitrage: the simultaneous buying or selling of assets in different markets to take advantage of difference in pricing for the same product.
74 Guo, X. (2008). "The Fall of Long-Term Capital Management." *Lingnan Journal of Banking, Finance and Economics,*

1. Retrieved from http://commons.ln.edu.hk/ljbfe/vol1/iss1/1

75 Ibid.

76 Amadeo, "Bailout."

77 Peters, Basil. *Early Exits: Exit Strategies for Entrepreneurs and Angel Investors (but Maybe Not Venture Capitalists).* Coquitlam, B.C.: MeteorBytes, 2009.

78 Palmer, Annie. "Jeff Bezos Is Now Worth More than $200 Billion." CNBC, August 26, 2020, www.cnbc.com/2020/08/26/amazon-ceo-jeff-bezos-worth-more-than-200-billion.html.

79 Calculated with data from Private Domestic—Price Indices by Class (Territory-Wide). *Hong Kong Property Review Monthly Supplement.* Hong Kong Government Rating and Valuation Department, 2019.